THE BAKER'S DIARY

Life in Georgian England
from the Book of George Sloper,
a Wiltshire baker, 1753 – 1810

PAMELA COLMAN

WILTSHIRE COUNTY COUNCIL,
LIBRARY & MUSEUM SERVICE
and
WILTSHIRE ARCHAEOLOGICAL AND
NATURAL HISTORY SOCIETY

ACKNOWLEDGEMENTS

My thanks go to the Wiltshire Archaeological and Natural History Society for allowing me to make use of the original manuscript held in the Society's Library.

Dr. James Thomas of Portsmouth Polytechnic offered invaluable help and encouragement as did Edward Bradby who compiled the index.

I am deeply indebted to Mrs. Barbara Fuller who transcribed so much of the original diary and to my son Ralph Colman and my good friend Stephen Beaumont for the most precious stimulus, guidance and enduring support.

Also I extend my thanks to Daphne Robinson and Derek Parker without whose help with typing and photography this book would never have been finished.

THE BAKER'S DIARY

Cover illustration: front; first page of George Sloper's diary
back; extract from Edward Dore's map of Devizes 1759

A NOTE ON QUOTATIONS AND REFERENCES

Any quotation not given a reference is taken from George Sloper's book. Sloper's colleagues on the borough council and other local persons are not referenced in the text but noted in the Prosopography.

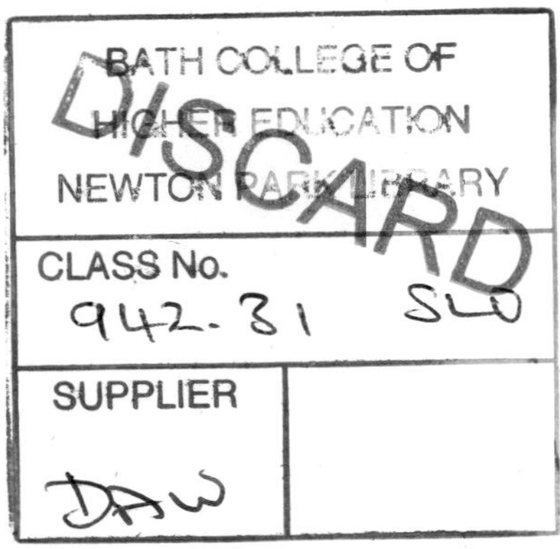

Published by Wiltshire County Council, Library & Museum Service and Wiltshire Archaeological and Natural History Society
Bythesea Road, Trowbridge, Wiltshire BA14 8BS
W.A.N.H.S. Charity Commission No. 309534

Printed by Wiltshire County Council Printing Department

1991

I.S.B.N. 0 86080 221 3

Geo: Sloper's Book

Devizes: Jany 1: 1753

My Father Came to live in this house (his & now my Dwelling)
& took a Lease – at Six pounds ℔ year in — 1713

Father bought this his Dwelling house in — 1717

Brother Rich^d was put a Prentice to Isaac Knight
Woolsaler in the Year — 1731

Brother Edward was Put a Prentice to John Clark
Stone Maker in the Year — 1734

Sunday afternoon about Six oClock
June 30. 1751 there was five Young Persons
Drowned in Drews Pond

Viz 1 Josiah Durham
2 Robert Merritt
3 Robert Merritt's wife
4 Tylee her Sister
5

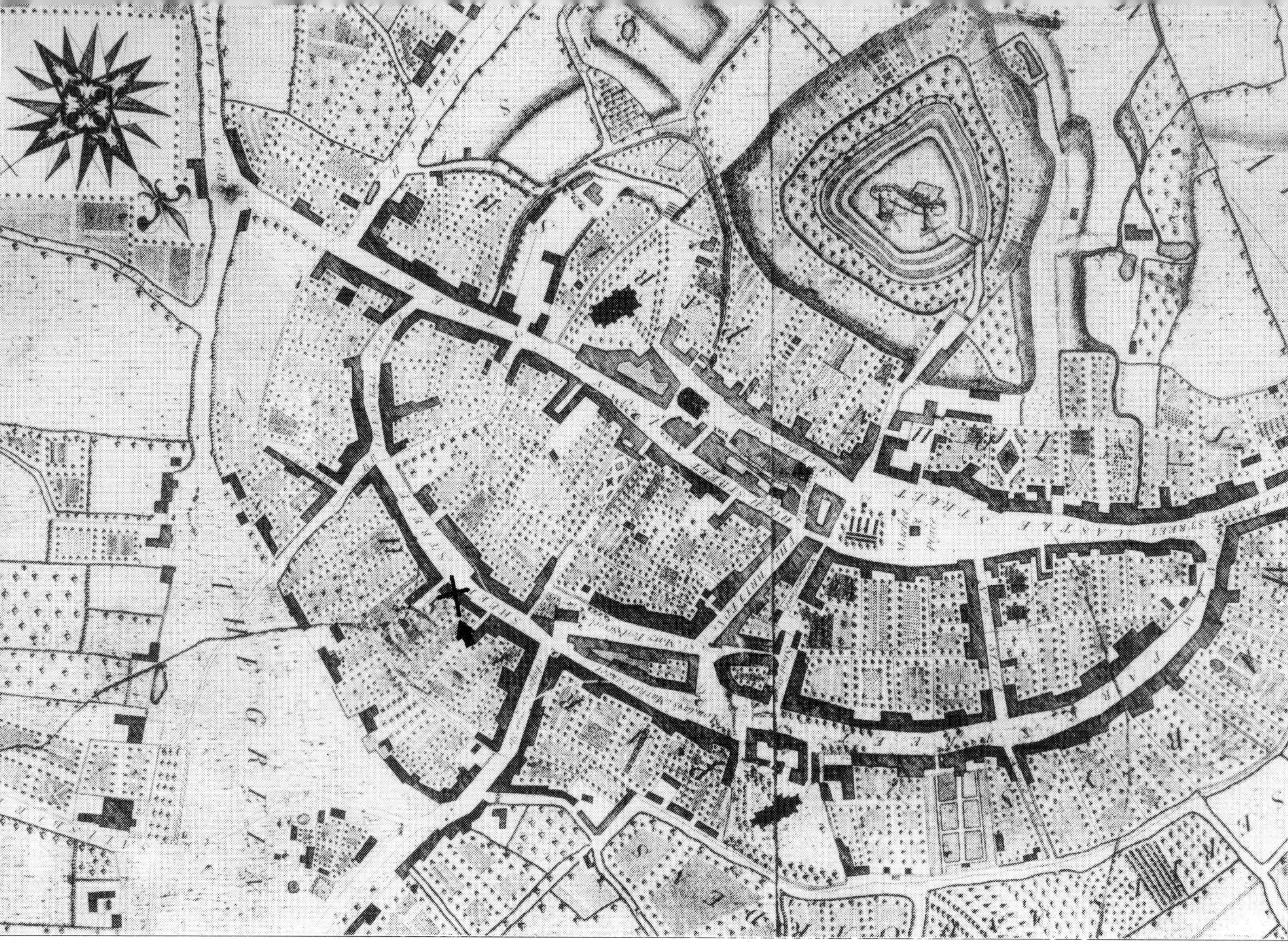

Extract from Edward Dore's map of Devizes, 1759. The position of Sloper's house in Sheep Street is indicated.

CONTENTS

ABBREVIATIONS

D.N.B.	*Dictionary of National Biography* (22 vols. 1921–22 reprint)
M.I.	Monuments and Monumental Inscriptions
Pa.	Parish
P.C.C.	Prerogative Court of Canterbury
P.R.O.	Public Record Office
V.C.H.	*Victoria County History*
W.A.M.	*Wiltshire Archaeological and Natural History Society Magazine*
W.A.N.H.S.	Wiltshire Archaeological & Natural History Society
W.R.S.	*Wiltshire Record Society*
W.R.O.	Wiltshire Record Office
W.N. & Q.	*Wiltshire Notes & Queries*

ILLUSTRATIONS

Foreword

Butchers, bakers, and candlestick makers were three of the essential tradesmen in towns, and yet as personalities in their communities they rarely emerge from the shadows. In this attractive account, Pamela Colman brings one of them to life. George Sloper, a baker of Devizes in the second half of the eighteenth century, who left an unusual book recording events in his public life: together with his daily takings from bread baked during fifty years. Skilfully she paints a portrait of a respected tradesman and responsible public figure in the town, and thereby knits together national and local events with a baker's mundane routine, kneading almost one hundred and fifty loaves each day. Sloper hardly ever betrayed any personal feelings in his writings, and yet a sympathetic human being emerges at the end, convivial, evidently popular, and far from lacking in concern for the poor.

A baker at work from 1753 to 1802 was providing a vital foodstuff at a time when the expanding population began once more to place severe strains on grain supplies. This narrative shows clearly the tight connection between Sloper's personal business and the temper of life in the town. Occasionally Sloper saw bread prices rise to crisis levels when the harvests failed; his was then the responsibility to be among the first to respond in a positive way. Plainly his life was inseparable from the life of all the townsfolk. And though he accumulated enough wealth to have turned himself into a country gentleman, had he so wished, he plainly preferred to bake, mill, and brew as long as his strength endured, and to reside nowhere else but in Devizes.

George Sloper's family history over several generations also reveals, or implies, some threads of continuity in the philosophical outlook of its members. In the Cromwellian period, a Sloper accepted the office of mayor, while George's nephew in 1808 was "the energetic founder of congregationalism in Devizes". George himself was a Tory, but with an independent spirit that led him to tolerate religious dissent, and to move in his later years towards support for the Whiggish viewpoint. He died too soon, however, to show his hand during the campaign for electoral reform which culminated in the act of 1832.

The many insights of this sensitively written book will be much appreciated by local historians of towns, and not least by those who are now zestfully exploring the ramifications of family dynasties.

Joan Thirsk

Diaries, no matter with what centuries they are concerned, are among the most valuable sources for the historian, and of equal value whether or not they were originally intended for eventual publication. Some are concerned with great events, others with the routines of life.

Source: J. Munson (ed.), T*he Diary of the Reverend Andrew Clark* (Oxford, 1988).
Foreward by Asa Briggs

Throughout the text monetary values are given in pounds, shillings and pence. Readers are reminded that the shilling became 5 new pence while an old penny equates to about 0.42 new pence. A guinea was 21 shillings (£1.05).

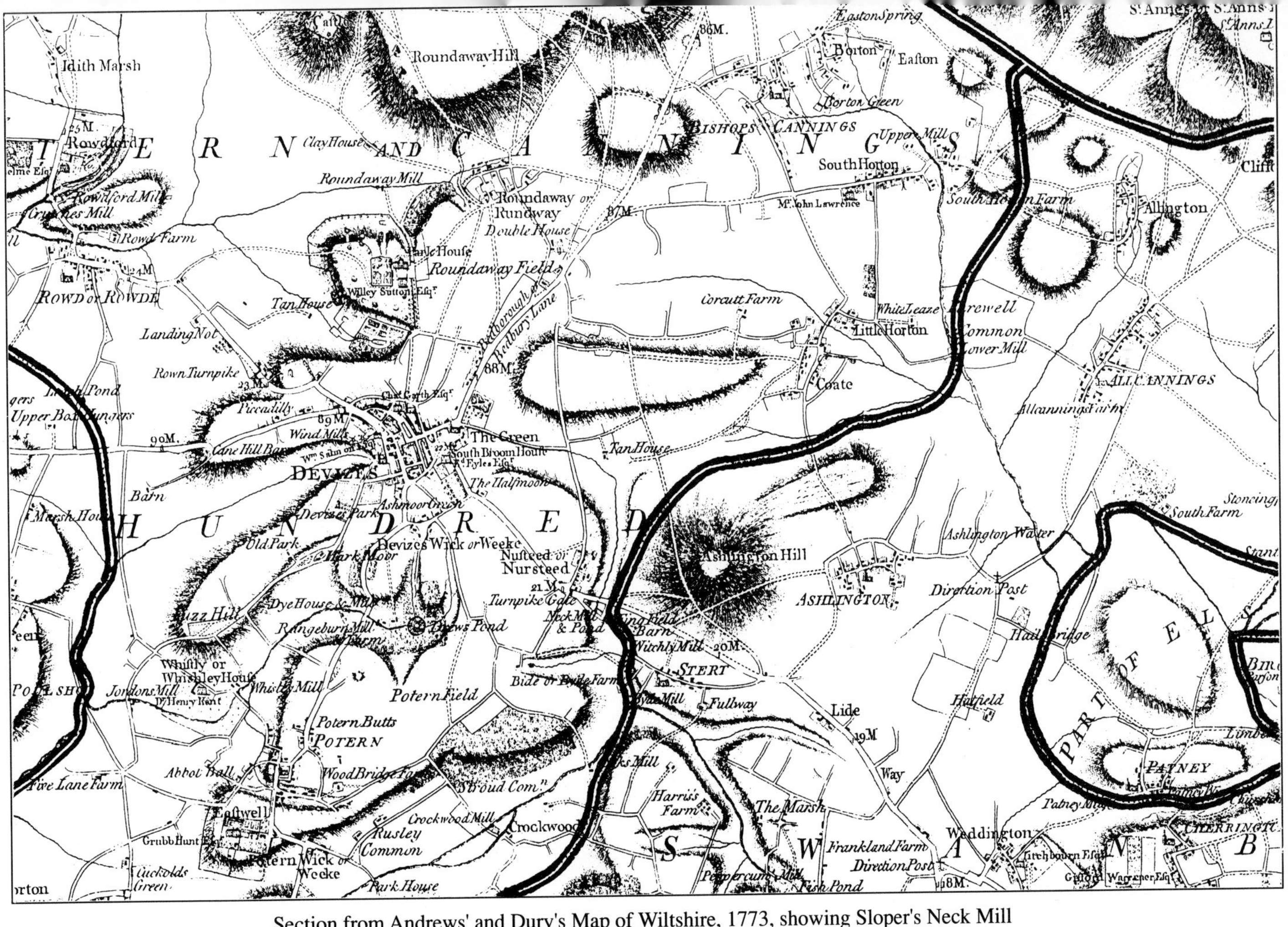

Section from Andrews' and Dury's Map of Wiltshire, 1773, showing Sloper's Neck Mill at Stert to the south east of Devizes, Scale 1¹/₈ inches to 1 mile.

The Church of St. Mary has some Norman work and a fine nave with a clerestory. The tower is 15th century and has 6 bells, the earliest dates from 1663.

The Church of St. John is contemporary with the first stone castle of Devizes built by Bishop Roger of Salisbury in 1120. The chancel, transept and tower of the church are the original Norman building.

I Introduction

The Wiltshire community of Devizes, on its wide downland expanse, was a new creation, starting life as the urban satellite to the great castle of a twelfth century founder.[1] A prosperous town developed, becoming a natural trading place for a large central part of the county. The outer bailey of Devizes Castle swept eastwards on a wide, gentle curve. Within that space, the church of St. John served the needs of the garrison; outside it was St. Mary's, the people's church, adjoining the spacious bustling Market Place. The inhabitants valued themselves as being royal tenants, with one of the best markets in England. John Leland wrote that 'the "beauty" of it was all in one strete'.[2] It is to be presumed that he thus refers to the short thoroughfare of The Brittox, still Devizes' main shopping street, which, in the days of the medieval castle, was aligned to the direction of a bretesque or timbered gate tower.

The economy of Devizes in the eighteenth century was dependent on its central position in Wiltshire and its markets for agricultural products. Wool was important at the beginning of the period, when there was a Guild of Merchants in addition to the Mayor and Corporation.[3] By the middle of the century, however, the Guild was of no more significance than a club for conviviality. A local historian, writing in 1859, recorded that the cloth manufacturing trade, once carried on by six or seven establishments, did not leave Devizes entirely until 1830, and that these could offer employment for near one thousand persons. Of these establishments, the most notable was that of John Anstie, who in 1785 built a 'manufactory', just off the Market Place. The principal manufactures of the town and district were serges, cashmeres and broad-cloths. In 1739 there were riots caused by the merchants buying up wool for export, leaving little for the spinners and weavers in their own houses.[4]

Such local government as existed was in the hands of the Mayor and Burgesses, operating under medieval charters regranted in the Jacobean period.[5] The Corporation consisted of a Mayor, Recorder, ten Capital Burgesses and twenty-four common councilmen, who had the liberty of making whatever number of Burgesses they pleased.

The powers of the Mayor and Burgesses were limited in some ways. They had, for example, no power to levy a rate, relying instead on their income from municipally owned property, the tolls from exclusive rights granted by their charters to hold markets for agricultural produce, of which wool was the most important, from fines for agricultural produce, of which wool was also the most important, from fines on their members for non-attendance at Council meetings, and refusal to accept the Mayoral office. The total income from these sources was not great, some £350 per annum, and not subject to much variation. The Corporation's most important task was electing members to Parliament, a function exercised almost continuously since 1295 A.D. By Tudor times the Borough regularly sent two members to Westminster, and by Sloper's time it was well established that all Burgesses could vote. By the time of the 1832 Reform Act, the total voting strength of the Corporation was just over 30 and the Burgesses were careful to keep the numbers small.[6] The Corporation was also empowered to hold its own Quarter Sessions and to elect its own Recorder to preside when the Court sat. This office usually went to a lawyer, who would later become one of the borough's Members of Parliament, and its most distinguished holder was Henry Addington, Borough Member and Recorder from 1784, when he was 27 years of age; he held the Recordership until 1828. He became Speaker of the House of Commons in 1789, was created Viscount Sidmouth after disagreement with William Pitt, whom he temporarily succeeded as Prime Minister from 1801 to 1804.[7] The Corporation also administered a considerable number of charities, including the 'Coventry Dole', involving distribution of a halfpenny loaf on a certain day to all inhabitants, and a penny loaf to all wayfarers.[8]

The parishes of the two churches of St. Mary the Virgin and St. John the Baptist, both of Norman foundation, were together co-extensive with the Borough. The Mayor and Corporation had special pews in both churches, and the more prosperous citizens monopolised the remainder of the sittings. It is not surprising, therefore, that in the 1770s large crowds of manual workers gathered to hear John Wesley's open-air preaching. It was not unknown for citizens to attend St. John's or St. Mary's in the morning and hear Presbyterian or Methodist preachers in the afternoon.[9]

The Georgian period saw the building of many elegant houses in Devizes, but there was still no piped water supply and only a rudimentary drainage system. However the Turnpike Trusts, the earliest in 1706 but many more by the 1750s and, in the 1780s, the Devizes Improvement Commissioners started to improve the town's roads and sanitation.[10]

With its position on one of the highways to the West of England, and with better transport, Devizes soon became a major stopping place on the way from London to the West, and this meant much more business for the four principal coaching inns. Three stage coaches stopped at *The Bear*

Henry Addington, first Viscount Sidmouth, was a man of great influence in Devizes. He was Prime Minister from 1801-1804 and Recorder of Devizes from 1784-1828.

Drawing of Devizes Market Cross which was built in 1814 using £1500 given by Henry Addington, Viscount Sidmouth.

James I added new charter rights including entitlement to name "The Mayor and Burgesses of the Borough of Devizes'.

1987 The Corporate Seal of the Borough of Devizes. George Sloper was Mayor in 1781, 1791 and 1800.
▼

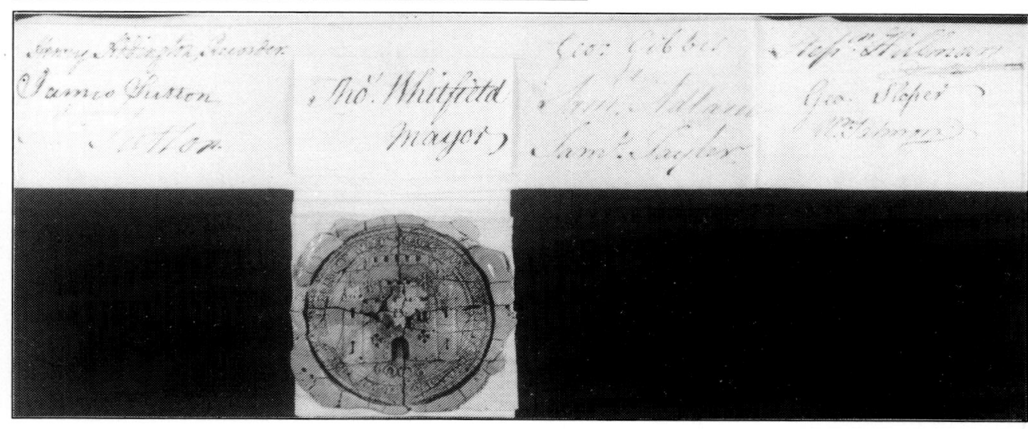

every morning and evening on their way to Bath. In the 1770s guests who stayed there might come away with charming pastel portraits quickly done for them by young Thomas Lawrence, later Sir Thomas Lawrence, P.R.A., the landlord's son.[11] Waggons for merchandise passed from London to Devizes on Tuesday, Thursday and Saturday. No doubt this traffic brought some economic advantage to the town, as did the Kennet and Avon Canal which opened at the beginning of the century.[12] But no major industry found a home in Devizes after its wool and cloth trade left the district. A new trade did, however, quickly expand in the town, and was to be a feature for the next 200 years – the preparation of tobacco and manufacture of snuff.[13]

References

1. *V.C.H. Wiltshire*, 14 Vols. (1953–91), Vol.X, p.225.
2. J. Waylen, *A History, Military and Municipal of the Ancient Borough of the Devizes* (Devizes 1859), p.101.
3. *Ibid.*, p.399.
4. *Ibid.*, p.398.
5. B. H. Cunnington, *Some Annals of the Borough of Devizes; being a Series of Extracts from the Corporation Records 1535–1835*, (2 Vols. Devizes 1925–6), Vol.1, p.152.
6. J. Waylen, op cit., p.578.
7. *V.C.H. Wiltshire*, Vol.X., p.178.
8. B. H. Cunnington, op. cit., Vol.1, p.12.
9. J. Waylen, op. cit., p.380.
10. *V.C.H. Wiltshire*, Vol.X, p.12.
11. J. Waylen, op. cit., p.378. Thomas Lawrence (1769–1830) at age 12 had his studio in Bath (after his father left *The Bear*, in financial difficulties). At 18 he was a student at the Royal Academy. At 20 he painted Queen Charlotte, consort of George III. Said to be remarkable for its maturity and one of his best works, the painting now hangs in the National Portrait Gallery. Royal Academician in 1794, he was knighted 1815 and was president of the Royal Academy 1820. He was considered to be the favourite portrait painter of the time.
12. K. R. Clew, *The Kennet and Avon Cana*l (Newton Abbot, 1985), p.73.
13. B. H. Cunnington, op. cit., Vol.1, p.112.

II Sloper the Man

'I will make a prief of it in my notebook'

Hugh Evans in the *Merry Wives of Windsor*, Act I, Scene I.

In the Library of the Wiltshire Archaeological and Natural History Society at Devizes is the book of George Sloper. A Master Baker, born in 1730, he meticulously recorded, between the ages of 23 and 72, his daily takings for bread which he sold in this ancient market town where he spent his entire ninety-year life. The book provides an insight into municipal affairs in a 'close' borough of some 3,500 inhabitants in the days before the Reform Act of 1832, and into the craft of breadmaking. It illustrates the separate activities of borough, parish vestry and, after 1781, improvement commissioners, as well as the impact of a rising cost of living on the working class. As the years passed Sloper also used it for recording international, national, regional, business and personal matters.

Three years before Sloper was born George II had come to the throne. As a boy Sloper would learn of 'the 45'[1] and hear of, if indeed he was not present as a seventeen-year old, the riots caused by John Wesley preaching in 1747.[2] He would see the decline of the Wiltshire woollen industry,[3] the publication of the first Devizes newspaper in 1752 and, ten years later, the opening of the town's first bank.[4] He would also see the rise of the Devizes snuff industry under the Ludlows, Leaches and Ansties.[5] Abroad there would be almost continuous war with France, the French Revolution, and the seemingly interminable struggle with Napoleon. He mentioned Quebec's capture by General James Wolfe, and the loss of the American colonies, side by side with the daily life of Devizes which he keenly observed and recorded. He lived through most of George II's reign, the whole 60 years of George III and just one year of George IV. He served three times as Mayor, eight years as Chamberlain, and became 'the father of the Corporation'. When writing as an old man Sloper recorded:

> 2 Aug 1810. Memorandum that I was this day 80 years old and was born Tuesday July 21 1730 Old Style. The Old Style ended Sept. 2nd 1752 and the next day was called Sept. 14th.

Governmental decree being unpopular in certain quarters, old men of the time used to say that they had been robbed of twelve days.[6] This change in the calendar was bound to cause difficulties. The then new style of measuring time, devised by Pope Gregory XIII, was statutorily introduced to the United Kingdom in 1752, as Sloper says. He tends to use the 'old style' for recording family events before that date, thus 'Bro. Ben was married at Holt ... Dec. 11 1751, ye old style'.

The Slopers of Devizes and its vicinity cannot be said to have been 'landed', or of that affluent merchant class which, in Georgian times, itself became landed. They were not gentry, but of that somewhat indefinable group 'yeoman', assuming that this includes locally successful tradesmen. The Slopers were well established in Devizes for 150 years before George Sloper's birth. Thus in 1570, Richard and Elizabeth Sloper sold 70 acres at Urchfont, four miles from Devizes, known as 'Sloper's Hold', to Robert Noyes, of another old Devizes family.[7] Richard Sloper's paternal great-grandfather, John, a successful tradesman, was Mayor of Devizes in 1651 and 1658 during the Commonwealth period, and again in 1668.[8] A Robert Sloper was Mayor in 1671 and 1672, having apparently been forgiven for calling two of his fellow magistrates knaves and fools, shaking his staff at the then Mayor and calling him an impudent rogue. Another Robert Sloper, Mayor in 1743, was Sloper's uncle. Sloper's father, Samuel, though never Mayor, was elected as a burgess and to the Common Council of Devizes, as was an elder brother, Richard, somewhat later.[9]

Sloper was the youngest of a family of eight, born to Samuel and his wife Mary, *née* Farmer. Samuel Sloper was born in 1691 and Mary in 1690, so his father and mother were both abut 40 when George was born. Samuel Sloper was a master baker, and successful enough to buy, in 1717, his rented house at the corner of Sheep Street and Hare and Hounds Street in Devizes. (See map on page 6). 'Father came to live in this house, now my dwelling, and took a lease of £6 a year in 1713,' and 'Father bought this, his dwelling house, in 1717,' wrote Sloper in his record. The bakehouse adjoined the house which, in Victorian times, was known as Number 29, Sheep Street. Both are now demolished.

Samuel Sloper, the master-baker, was in 1727 elected a burgess of Devizes, and later 'sworn of the Common Council', a position his son was to attain fifty years later. Both father and son were churchwardens at St. Mary's church. His father lived to be 80, Sloper recording, 'My father Samuel Sloper dyed Saturday morning November 30 aged 80 years and about five months 1771'. And he dutifully paid for the funeral,[10] noting;

Father's funeral – 3rd December 1771		
To lime	...	£0 4s. 0d.
Paid for coffin	...	£3 1s. 6d.
Mr. Neat for crape	...	£5 14s. 4d.
Mr. George Hillier	...	£1 2s. 3d.
do	...	£3 4s. 10d.
To Mr. R. Read	...	£10 3s. 6d.
To Mr. Whitfield	...	£10 9s. 4d.
To Hamlingford – Cuttler	...	£0 3s. 3d.
To Painter for bricking the grave	...	£0 13s. 4d.
To I. Cleeve, Sexton	...	£0 10s. 0d.
		£35 5s. 5d.

Sloper's entry for his mother's death in 1756 was heavily scored by a double line – 'my mother, Mary Sloper, dyed Thursday, November 25 1756, aged 66 years and upwards.'

George Sloper's elder brothers were Richard, born 1716, elected a Councilman in 1765; Edward, born in 1718; Samuel, who died young; and Benjamin, born 1723 and referred to by George in his diary as 'Bro. Ben'. George Sloper appears to have been closer to Benjamin than to the others and also to Benjamin's son, the Reverend Robert Sloper, the energetic founder of congregationalism in Devizes; he made the latter's son, George Elgar Sloper, his heir. Of George Sloper's three sisters, Ann died unmarried at 26, Ruth made two marriages and Mary one – to John Rose, a farmer. The marriages, deaths and births of the children of the two married sisters were duly recorded. Of sister Ruth's funeral, for which he clearly paid,[11] he wrote;

March 7 1783		
To post chaise of Halcomb to Stowford March 2nd	...	£1 1s. 0d.
Turnpike and driver	...	£0 3s. 6d.
To Hill – Cuttler	...	£0 3s. 6d.
To Briscott	...	£0 0s. 10d.
To Robert Greenland for bricking the grave 9 inch thick	...	£0 16s. 0d.
To ditto for beer	...	£0 1s. 0d.
To Rob. West for 11½ inch handbrick	...	£1 7s. 9d.
To Sexton of St. Mary's for	...	£0 6s. 8d.
To ye clark for carrying of hatbands	...	£0 2s. 6d.

George Sloper's house in Sheep Street and Hare and Hounds Street showing the bakehouse chimney on the far right.

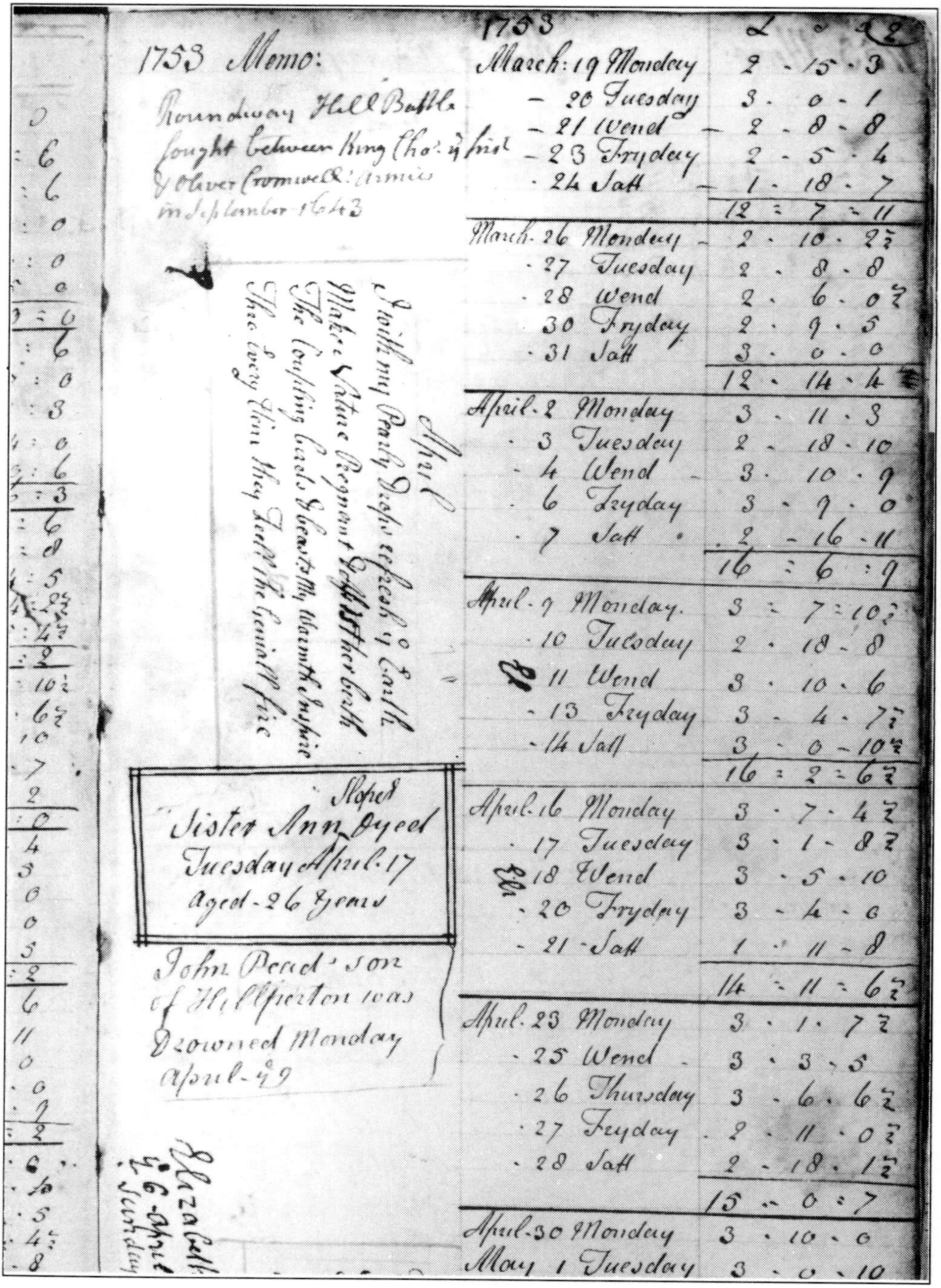

1753 Memo:

Roundway Hill Battle fought between King Chas ye first & Oliver Cromwell's Armies in September 1643

Sloper
Sister Ann Dyed
Tuesday April 17
Aged 26 years

John Pead' son of Hillperton was Drowned Monday April 9

1753			
March 19 Monday	2	15	3
20 Tuesday	3	0	1
21 Wend	2	8	8
23 Fryday	2	5	4
24 Satt	1	18	7
	12	7	11
March 26 Monday	2	10	2½
27 Tuesday	2	8	8
28 Wend	2	6	0½
30 Fryday	2	9	5
31 Satt	3	0	0
	12	14	4
April 2 Monday	3	11	3
3 Tuesday	2	18	10
4 Wend	3	10	9
6 Fryday	3	9	0
7 Satt	2	16	11
	16	6	9
April 9 Monday	3	7	10½
10 Tuesday	2	18	8
11 Wend	3	10	6
13 Fryday	3	4	7½
14 Satt	3	0	10½
	16	2	6½
April 16 Monday	3	7	4½
17 Tuesday	3	1	8½
18 Wend	3	5	10
20 Fryday	3	4	6
21 Satt	1	11	8
	14	11	6½
April 23 Monday	3	1	7½
25 Wend	3	3	5
26 Thursday	3	6	6½
27 Fryday	2	11	0½
28 Satt	2	18	1½
	15	0	7
April 30 Monday	3	10	0
May 1 Tuesday	3	0	10

The start of George Sloper's baking record in March 1753.

To Cleeve, Sexton of St. John's for grave and bell	...	£0 11s.	6d.
To Mr. Mayo bands and gloves	...	£8 19s.	3d.
To Mr. Whitfield's bill for Bands Paull and Gloves	...	£5 10s.	0d.

The house in which Sloper and his brothers and sisters were born, and in which he was to spend his whole life, was substantial and he noted;

1764 July 23 – New paved the bakehouse and portch with Swindon stone

1765 Feb. 26 – Enlarged and wenscoted the Parlour.

1772 April 6 – New flowered cotton bed in ye best chamber.

There must have been at least four bedrooms – one for his parents, one for the boys, one for the girls and one for a female domestic. Sloper remained a bachelor, but his diary entries show his interest in his family and their doings, and in his house.

The diary gives no hint of Sloper's life up to the age of 23 when, in 1753, he began, in a meticulously neat hand, to list the daily takings for the sale of bread he had baked in the Sheep Street bakehouse adjoining the family residence. No particulars of his schooling appear. It could be safely inferred, however, that his father, master baker, houseowner and councilman, had sufficient means to pay for his education locally. Devizes Corporation had provided a schoolhouse by 1719 and employed a schoolmaster, paying him an income from various small charities. By 1725 the Corporation had built a new schoolhouse which, under the name of the Free School, existed to within a few years of 1800. It appointed schoolmasters in 1733 and 1737, the latter being the year in which Sloper, then seven years old, may be presumed to have begun his formal education with possible instruction in penmanship, English, arithmetic, accounts, geography, use of the globes and drawing.[12] The balance of probability is that Sloper attended this school. He was certainly taught to be painstaking and accurate, and his book in the early years is a model of neatness, though as he grew older it became less tidy. Sloper's father would pay fees for his son's education direct to the schoolmaster. However, like many of his contemporaries, he never learnt to spell and his English is deplorable. Thus against the date 1751, he wrote:

There was five young persons drowned in Drews Pond.

and in a recipe;

Good for a cold – Serup of Vilets
Serup of Roses
Serup of Lemons
Serup of Colts Foot
Oyl of Almonds
Hony
Of each one pennyworth.

Stranger still was his mis-spelling of the two commodities with which he was most closely concerned – flour was 'flower', and loaf was 'lofe'. It should, however, be borne in mind that spelling was not standardised in Sloper's youth and Dr. Johnson's dictionary was not published until 1755. Variations in spelling are not therefore a sign of illiteracy.

It is unlikely that Sloper stayed at school beyond the age of sixteen, when he would be of the normal age for seven-year apprenticeship. Given the financial demands of apprenticeship Sloper's father would feel it a waste of money to apprentice his son to anyone when he could teach him his trade himself.[13]

Between the age of twenty-three and thirty-eight, when he first received public office under the Corporation as 'Mayor's Constable', George Sloper set the pattern of notes which he continued until he was over eighty. He was certainly concise in style, generally content to note facts without moralizing about them, keeping his opinions to himself. His notes may be grouped under family, local, national and international events. As to the family, as well as births, marriages and deaths, items of health interested him. 'Bro. Ben' had pleurisy and his father 'is very bad in the gout' and broke his ribs by a fall at a public house. He himself was, in January 1757, 'very ill in the fever'. But most of notes on health matters relate to the contemporary scourge of smallpox. In 1761 1,266 cases were counted in Devizes out of a population of about 3,100 and 80 of these were fatal.[14] In 1875 he recorded three deaths from smallpox. In 1794 'a general ocolation for the small pox began' and he had his 'servant boy innoculated'.

In 1764 Sloper 'was drawn for to go a Militiaman, gave James Phillips one guinea to be a substitute'. The Militia was organised for home defence on a county basis under the Lord Lieutenant. A baker was not sufficiently high in the social scale to be offered a commission, and service in the ranks would be most uncongenial.[15] It was not a popular

A

TREATISE

ON THE

ANANAS

OR

PINE-APPLE,

Containing plain and eafy Directions for raifing this

Moft excellent FRUIT *without Fire, and in much higher Perfection*

Than from the STOVE.

Illuftrated with an elegant Copper Plate, in which is exibited, the new invented PINE-FRAME, &c. peculiarly adapted for that Ufe; with another, fhewing the Fruit colour'd from Nature.

To which are added, full Directions for raifing MELONS.

By ADAM TAYLOR Gardener near *Devizes.*

DEVIZES:

Printed by T. BURROUGH, for the Author,

And Sold by *Meff.* ROBINSON *and* ROBERTS, *in Pater-Nofter-Row*; Mr. ROBSON, *in New Bond Street*; Mr. ROSE, No. 2 *Goodge Street, Oxford-Road, London*; *Meff.* PALMER *and* BECKET, *in Briftol*; *Mr.* FREDERICK, *in Bath*; *Mr.* EASTON, *in Salif-bury*; *Meff.* MERRILLS, *in Cambridge*; *Mr.* PACK *and Mr.* TESSYMAN, *in York*; *Mr.* SLACK, *in Newcaftle*; *Mr.* BAKER, *Tunbridge*; *Meff.* FLACTONS, *in Canterbury*; *Meff.* TOFT *d* LOBB, *in Chelmsford*; *Mr.* SILVER, *in Sandwich*; T. BUR-UGH, *in Devizes*; *By all other* BOOKSELLERS, *and the* THOR. M DCCLXIX.

▲

Title page of *A Treatise on the Ananas or Pine-apple*. Written by a local man this is one of the books which George Sloper noted in his diary.

Robert Sloper, Dissenting Minister, b. 1758 d. 1818. Son of Benjamin Sloper and nephew of George Sloper.

The Devizes Bear Club was formed in 1756. One of its activities was the upkeep of a charity school, started in 1757. The aim of the foundation was that a boy "shall receive a plain English education such as may qualify him for a mechanical trade" Regular church attendance was one of the school rules.

Each boy received annually a coat, waist-coat, pair of trousers and a cap. These buttons were part of the uniform.

On leaving school (after four years) the club supervised the apprenticeship of the boys.

DEVIZES 23 *July* 1804.

BEAR CLUB.

THE Annual Meeting of this Club will be held on *Friday* the 17th day of *August* next, at which the Attendance of the Members is requeſted.

W. SALMON Steward.

☞ *Dinner at three o'Clock preciſely.*

Mr Geo: Sloper

George Sloper's invitation to the Bear Club Feast of 1804

service and it was both legal and common for professional and middle classes to find substitutes in this way and, owing to the economic condition of the labouring class, substitutes could always be found. Thus in 1809 the Wiltshire Militia Regiment, embodied since 1793, had only 50 other-rank volunteers, 102 serving under the ballot and the large majority, 619, balloted but finding substitutes.[16] That year Sloper noted '15 May – local Militia came to Devizes for 28 for ye first time'. Sloper, though he does not mention it, might wish they had not as on 6 June a mutiny broke out; the officers lost control and took refuge in *The Bear*. The situation was only saved by the appearance of the Yeomanry Cavalry officered, it is true, by the local gentry but filling its ranks with respectable volunteer yeomen and farmers who provided their own horses.[17] It is probable that Sloper had little interest in personal military service, despite his recording the victories of Wolfe, Nelson and Wellington. However, when another local defence force called the Devizes Loyal Volunteers, was formed owing to the Napoleonic threat in 1798, he noted:

> 1799 Sept. 16. The coulers was presented to the Devizes Volentiers on Roundway Down by Miss Sutton and Mrs. Addington wife to Mr. Addington, the Speaker of the House of Commins.

Many respectable citizens joined this defence force in the ranks,though at 69 Sloper was too old for involvement.

As a young man Sloper joined the Gardeners and Bear Clubs. Edward Dore's map (page 6) shows the rows of houses inside the curve of the town ditch, with their neat little gardens. Devizes gardener, Adam Taylor, wrote in 1769 *A Treatise on the Ananas, or, Pineapple*.[18] Sloper would remain a member of the Gardeners Club until its dissolution in 1810, when £6 8s. was returned to each of the then members. The Bear Club, of which Sloper's brother Benjamin was also a member, took its name from *The Bear Inn* in the Market Place, where its members met. This Club had, and still has, a distinguished history in educational provision, though it did not eschew holding, as Sloper noted, its 'Annual Feast'. It was one of those institutions beloved of the Georgians, combining conviviality with philanthropy. By 1765, the year of the earliest extant steward's accounts, 10 boys were being educated and the schoolmaster was paid £6 a year. Some £2 19s. 1d. was spent on cloth for the boys' clothes to be made up locally with 'trimmings' and hats costing 17s. 6d. By 1814 the school was taking 30 boys, their 'hats' trimmed with lace, and it was apprenticing boys to town tradesmen, the master's fee being about £10. The Club members did themselves very well, in particular at their annual August feast, when, according to the Steward's accounts, turkey, venison and turtles were on the menu.[19]

When Sloper was twenty-nine an event occurred which caused considerable interest all over the country. This was the case of a schoolmaster convicted of murder. The diary entry reads:

> 1759. August 3 – Fryday. Eugene Aram was tryed and found guilty at York assizes for and of the murder of Daniel Clark, a shoemaker. N.B. A remarkable circumstance –

One reason it was so was because of Aram's undoubted ability – he is said to have had a vast knowledge of botany, heraldry, Chaldaic, Arabic and Gaelic – and secondly the length of the time between the murder and the trial.[20] Also mentioned, in 1760, was the execution of Earl Ferrers for killing his manservant, the last time that a member of the House of Lords was tried for murder by his peers and,[21] on a less dramatic note, '1761 Feb. 13. Beau Richard Nash Esq. died at Bath'. At the same time he recorded the death of David Garrick, the actor.[22] Nash would have been well known to anyone at that time who was in the least interested in fashion and design.[23]

Internationally this was the period of the Seven Years' War, the latter part of which the elder Pitt so ably conducted against the French. Sloper commented, in 1757, on the execution by shooting on board H.M.S. *Monarque* of the unfortunate Admiral Byng, the charge being neglect of duty in that he failed to support the British Fleet's attack on the French off Minorca.[24] In 1779 Captain James Cook's death in Hawaii caused Sloper great difficulty in spelling – he 'was killed at Owhyhee an island in the South Seas'.[25]

Sloper took the periodical *The Universal Magazine* and often quotes from it. His information on Byng's execution, for example, is from this source; he entered 'see particulars in Universal Mag. 20 Voll. 89 page and 136 page'.[26] In June 1794 he 'began taking in Josephus History of the Jews at 6d. per number weekly'.[27] He probably knew the works of Stukeley[28] and Davis[29] on Wiltshire history: for example, he gave a basically accurate summary of the Royalist Cavalry victory at Roundway Down in 1643. Roundway Down lies 1 mile from Devizes, and Sloper would know the local tradition that the holes in the stonework at St. John's Church were said to be caused by cannon shot fired by the Roundheads when the town was under siege.

St. John's Alley, Devizes, showing the medieval hall on the right.

Price of wheat in Devizes Market
Jany 16th 1800

s d
Best wheat pr Bushill 13: 9
Second wheat pr Do 12-6
Third wheat. pr Do 11-8

E. Jordan

[illegible]

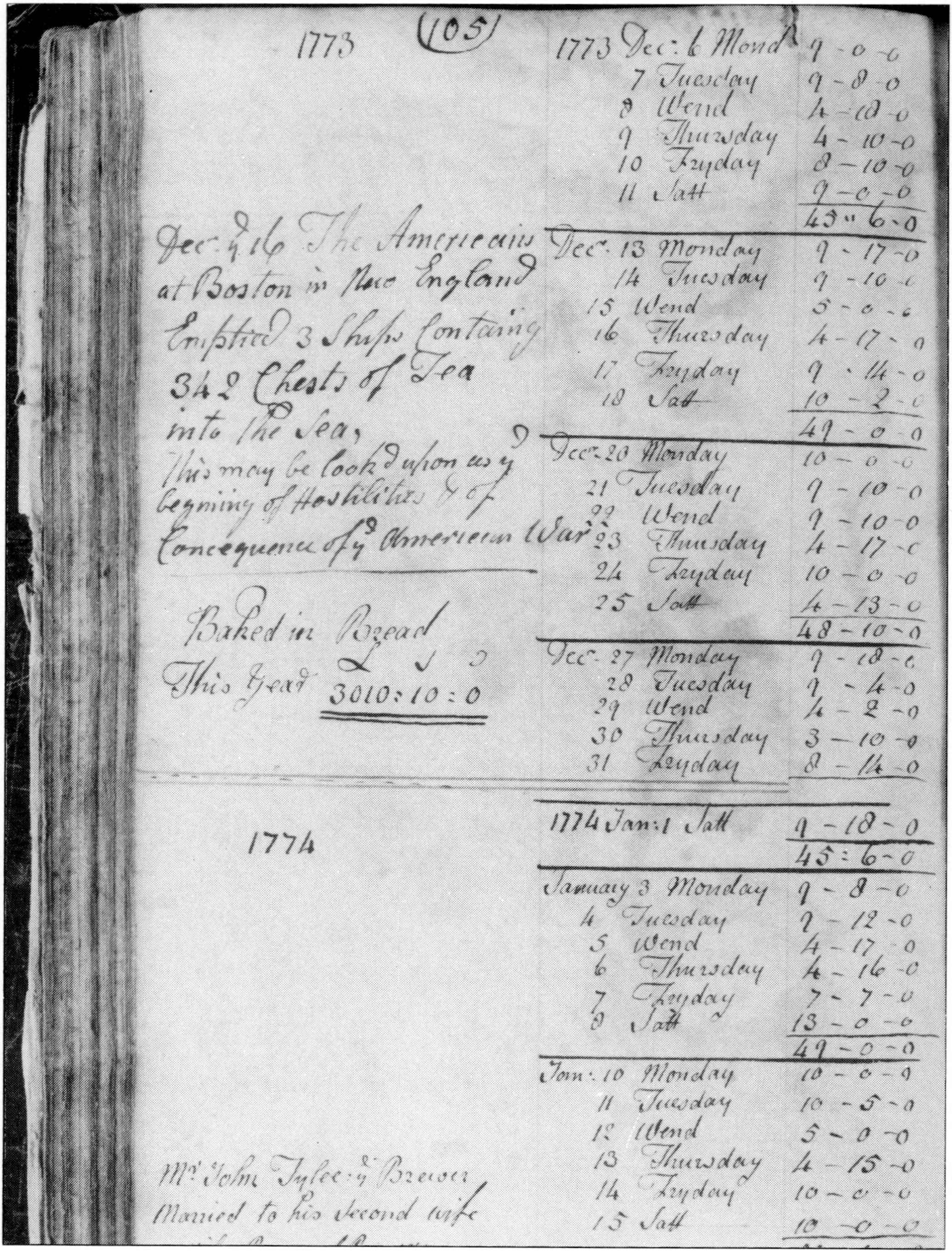

1773 (105)

Dec: ye 16 The Americans at Boston in New England Emptied 3 Ships Containing 342 Chests of Tea into the Sea,
This may be look'd upon as ye begining of Hostilities & of Conceqence of ye American War

Baked in Bread
This Year £ s d 3010:10:0

1773 Dec: 6	Mond	9 - 0 - 0
7	Tuesday	9 - 8 - 0
8	Wend	4 - 10 - 0
9	Thursday	4 - 10 - 0
10	Fryday	8 - 10 - 0
11	Satt	9 - 0 - 0
		45 " 6 - 0
Dec: 13	Monday	9 - 17 - 0
14	Tuesday	9 - 10 - 0
15	Wend	5 - 0 - 0
16	Thursday	4 - 17 - 0
17	Fryday	9 - 14 - 0
18	Satt	10 - 2 - 0
		49 - 0 - 0
Dec: 20	Monday	10 - 0 - 0
21	Tuesday	9 - 10 - 0
22	Wend	9 - 10 - 0
23	Thursday	4 - 17 - 0
24	Fryday	10 - 0 - 0
25	Satt	4 - 13 - 0
		48 - 10 - 0
Dec: 27	Monday	9 - 18 - 0
28	Tuesday	9 - 4 - 0
29	Wend	4 - 2 - 0
30	Thursday	3 - 10 - 0
31	Fryday	8 - 14 - 0
1774 Jan: 1	Satt	9 - 18 - 0
		45 : 6 - 0
January 3	Monday	9 - 8 - 0
4	Tuesday	9 - 12 - 0
5	Wend	4 - 17 - 0
6	Thursday	4 - 16 - 0
7	Fryday	7 - 7 - 0
8	Satt	13 - 0 - 0
		49 - 0 - 0
Jan: 10	Monday	10 - 0 - 0
11	Tuesday	10 - 5 - 0
12	Wend	5 - 0 - 0
13	Thursday	4 - 15 - 0
14	Fryday	10 - 0 - 0
15	Satt	10 - 0 - 0

1774

Mr John Tyler ye Brewer
Married to his second wife

In 1773 George Sloper records the Boston Tea Party.

In 1793 he reported a case of what he considered a miscarriage of justice:

> July 8. Thursday night. John Acorman of Pattney, ye baker and miller was robbed on Etchilhampton Hill above ye monument, a little across the old road and on Fryday James Sloper and Wm Coombes was taken up on suspision of ye above robbery and was committed by Charles Garth Esq to prison for the same but both declared themselves perfectly innocent. Tryed at Salisbury August 3 and by ye Jury was declared to be guilty and on August 17 they was both hanged and dyed very penitent, but both declared they was innocent of the crime which was a-going to die for and I sincerely and verily believe with all my Heart and Soul they was inocent.
> *Mem.* Since it has been found by the words of Rob. Franklin that his brother Thomas and John was the men that robbed Acorman.

Highwaymen were part of eighteenth century life, [30] as was avoiding import duties if at all possible. Thus Sloper noted:

> 1783. Dec 12. Smugglers to the number of 40 or more came to Devizes Fryday night between 11 and 12 clock at nyte and retook a large quantity of tea from Mr. Woods the Supervisor.

In 1784 he recorded that two Devizes men were tried and condemned for thefts of items worth less than £1 and transported to America for 7 years. Three years later he wrote:

> 1787. May 13. Sunday. Commodore Phillips sett sayle from Portsmouth for Bottney Bay with convicts for ye first time.[31]

The major international event of the 1770s and 1780s was the loss of the American colonies. Thus:

> 1773. Dec. the 16. The Americans at Boston in New England emptied 3 ships containing 342 chests of tea into the sea. This may be looked upon as the beginning of Hostilities and of consequence of the American War.

He also reported the Boston Tea Party as occurring on 15 December 1774 when the Americans 'throwed Tea in the sea'. The former year is correct, but Sloper tended to repeat himself, explicable perhaps by his noting events some time after they had happened. Of events abroad in the 1790s he wrote:

> 1793. Jan. Louis the Sixteenth, King of France, put to death by being beheaded ..... aged 38 years and 5 months in the 19th year of his reign

and

> Feb. 1. The French Convention declared war against England and Holland.

With the date given as July 14 1793 (the correct one is 13 July), Sloper wrote sideways on p. 199 of his record of the killing of Marat by Charlotte Corday:

> Marratt killed (stabd) by a woman at Paris .... a nobleman's daughter of Caen in Normandy. She was about 25 years old and is said very handsom .... she behaved at the place of execution with such boldness and courage that all the spectators was astonished and amazed.

He mentioned the Queen of France's execution on 16 October 1793, and those of the Duke of Orleans (Philip Egalite) on 7 November, the Princess Elizabeth the King's sister in May 1794 'by cutting off her head by the guillotine' and Madame du Barry 'misstress to Louis the 15' on 8 December. In America 'George Washington Esq. President of the Congress in North America gave his resignation. See his address to the people of America in the London Chronicle Vol. 80 – Nov. 10 1796, and 150 page'. The naval war with France received attention – 'in the Channel off Brest Admiral Lord Howe fought and beat the French Fleet', and 'Admiral Lord Nelson fought the French Fleet at Alexandria in Egypt, and took eight or nine men-of-war'. These actions are known as The Glorious First of June, and the Battle of the Nile. There was 'a general thanksgiving' for the latter, and no doubt a feast in the Town Hall. In India Tippo Sahib, son of Hyder Ali whom Coote had defeated in 1781, was giving trouble. Sloper wrote:

> The city of Seringapatam taken by storm ye 4 May 1779 and Tippo Sahib, the Prince or Sultan, Slain.[32]

Foreign news in the early 19th century was dominated by Napoleon,

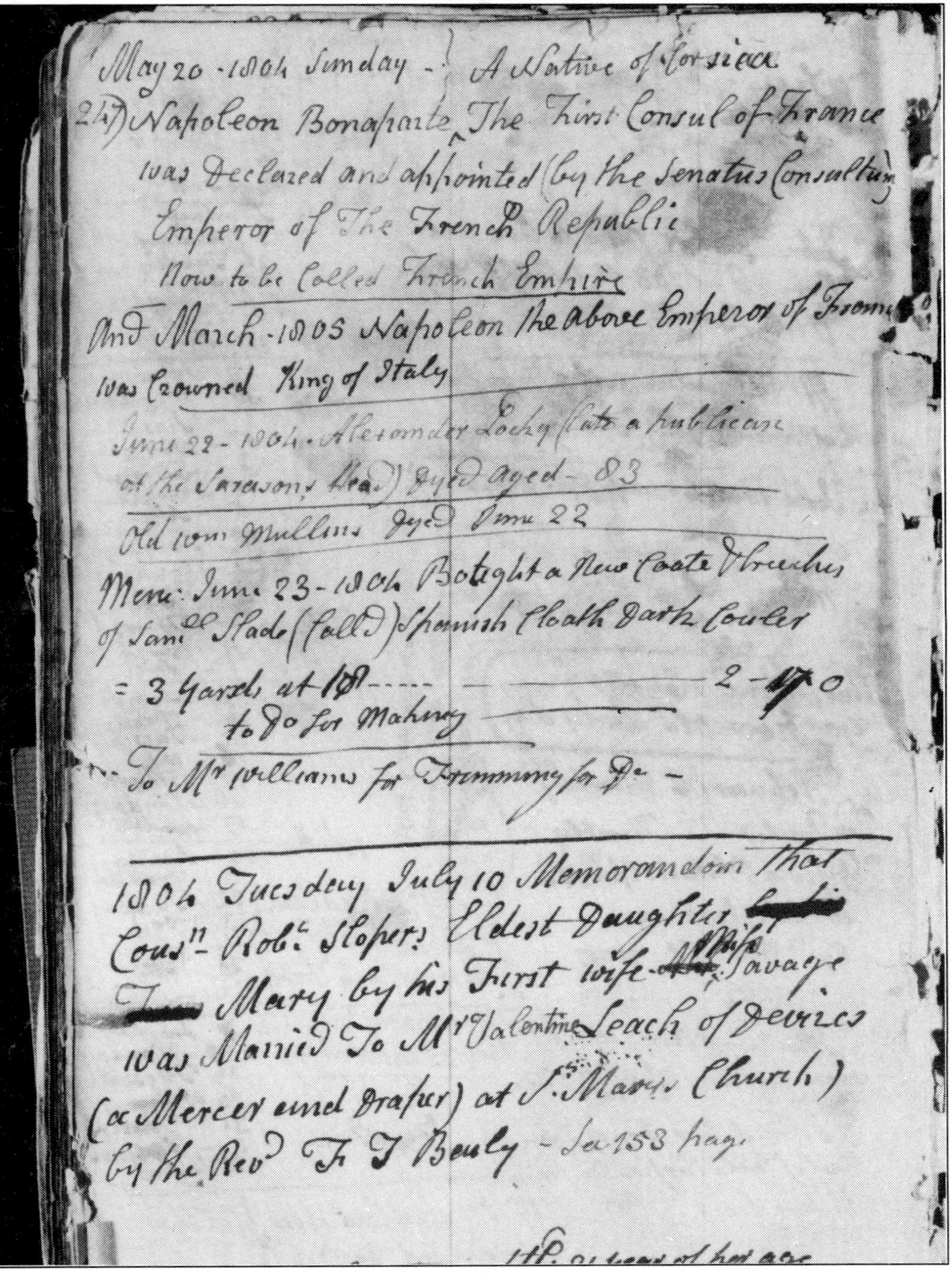

May 20 - 1804 Sunday - } A Native of Corsica
24) Napoleon Bonaparte, The First Consul of France
was Declared and appointed (by the Senatus Consultum)
Emperor of The French Republic
Now to be Called French Empire

And March - 1805 Napoleon the above Emperor of France
was Crowned King of Italy

June 22 - 1804 - Alexander Lockyer (late a publican
at the Saracens Head) Dyed aged - 83

Old Tom Mullins Dyed June 22

Mem: June 23 - 1804 Bought a New Coate & breeches
of Saml Slade (called) Spanish Cloath Dark Couler
= 3 Yards at 18/ ---- ———— 2 - 14 - 0
to Do for Making ————
To Mr Williams for Trimming for Do -

1804 Tuesday July 10 Memorandum that
Cousn. Robt. Slopers Eldest Daughter
Mary by his First wife Miss Savage
was Married To Mr Valentine Leach of Devizes
(a Mercer and Draper) at St Marys Church)
by the Revd F. T. Bouly - See 153 page

... 21 years of her age

On the same page that he noted Napoleon becoming emperor of France, Sloper records the wedding of his great-niece, Mary.

151 = 1782

Washed No 6
Nov: 4 & 5

Ed Hale dyed Thursday
Nov: 14

Brewed back — Filled
Nov: 19 – 12 – Adams filled Old Tom
" 26 – 12 [illegible] Scott No 5 –
Ale No 8 – 9 – 10 – 11
Old Tom 3 Pails [illegible]
No 5 – 5 Pails [illegible]

Mother dyed Nov: 25 – 1756
Father dyed Nov 30 – 1771

Richd Stevens Horton Dec 3
at 6 Pence a Week
Came to Live with me

Hyder Ally dyed this Month
at Serengapatam his Capitol
City in the East Indies (60)
& is Succeeded by his Son Tippoo
as Sultan (or King)

Washed Dec 16
(No 7)

Mr Bennett [illegible]
Silversmith dyed
Wednesday Dec: 18

Nov: 18	Monday	11 – 12 – 0
19	Tuesday	10 – 13 – 0
20	Wednesday	10 – 7 – 0
21	Thursday	5 – 4 – 0
22	Fryday	10 – 8 – 0
23	Satt	11 – 3 – 0
		59 . 7 . 0
Nov: 25	Monday	12 . 0 – 0
26	Tuesday	9 – 14 – 0
27	Wednesd	10 – 0 – 0
28	Thursd	5 – 10 – 0
29	Fryday	11 – 0 – 0
30	Satt	8 – 10 – 0
		56 .. 14 . 0
Decr 2	Mond	8 – 14 – 0
3	Tuesday	8 – 16 – 0
4	Wednesd	10 – 0 – 0
5	Thursday	4 – 15 – 0
6	Fryday	10 – 8 – 0
7	Satt	5 – 17 – 0
		48 . 10 . 0
Decr 9	Monday	14 . 1 . 0
10	Tuesday	9 – 5 – 0
11	Wednesd	10 – 12 – 0
12	Thursday	6 – 4 – 0
13	Fryday	11 – 7 – 0
14	Satt	12 – 1 – 0
		63 . 10 . 0
Dec: 16	Mond	10 – 13 – 0
17	Tuesday	9 – 6 – 0
18	Wed	10 – 2 – 0
19	Thursday	5 – 6 – 0
20	Fryday	10 – 3 – 0
21	Satt	11 – 0 – 0

Among a mixture of local and international news for 1782 Sloper notes that he washed No. 6 cask as part of his brewing activities.

and British political news by Addington and Pitt. On Napoleon and the French threat Sloper commented:

> May 20 1804. Napoleon Bonaparte, a native of Corsica, the first Consul of France was declared .... Emperor of the French Republic now to be called the French Empire, and March 1805 .... crowned 'King of Italy' – 'by the Pope'.

Nelson's victory at Trafalgar in October 1805, which destroyed 19 men-of-war of the combined fleets of France and Spain, is recorded and the burgesses organised a 'thanksgiving'. The 'great blody battle' of Jena in 1806, when of the Prussian Army '180,000 all killed and wounded and made prisoners' and 'in which the French gained a complete victory', and 'the Duke of Brunswick dyed – as is supposed of a broken heart', received full mention. By 1808 Wellington was in the Iberian Peninsula and there was better news – 'Aug. 17 the British Army in Portugal fought and beat the French .... and gained a complete victory near Lisbon'. Napoleon's marriage to 'the daughter of the Emperor of Germany aged 19', when he 'put away the Empress', suggests a note of disapproval. The record ceases before Waterloo in 1815.

The bakery business was prospering. In 1770 he could afford to buy a copper furnace, presumably for brewing as he reported making a fair quantity of ale in later years. A greater sign of his growing prosperity was his giving, in 1775, some £1,360 for an estate just outside the borough on the north-east, called 'Rotherstone'. He also held a copyhold estate at Coate and three houses at the junction of Bridewell Street and Morris Lane and so, by now, was a substantial man of property. On one occasion he recorded insuring a property against fire with the Royal Exchange Assurance Society, whose plaques can be seen to this day on Devizes houses.[33] A building at Coate was insured for £300 at a premium of 17s. 6d. He does not mention other insurances but could well have been a member of the Wiltshire Fire Insurance Company, founded in Devizes in 1784.[34]

As a prominent local tradesman and a leading member of the close Corporation at Devizes he took an interest in the national scene at Westminster. He could hear at first hand from the local Members of Parliament, Charles Garth and then Henry Addington in whose elections he played a part, what the Government and Opposition were thinking and doing. They came regularly to Devizes to sit as Recorders at Quarter Sessions or the Court of Records. Thus he mentioned the election of John Wilkes,[35] as Chamberlain of the City of London in 1779; the Gordon

Riots of 1780 – 'Great rabble at London called the Lord George Gordon's mob caused by an Act of Parliament being in favour of Popery',[36] and previously in 1771 'Brass Crosby Lord Mayor of London sent to the Tower by the House Commons'.[37] Sloper continued to note items of political interest:

> 1780. Jan 26 Wed. A County meeting at ye Town Hall pettition Parliament to Redress ye Grienvences of Pentioners and useless place-men. The principal speakers was –
>
> Erle of Shelbern
> Erle of Radnor
> Erle of Abington
> Hon. Chas Fox etc.[38]

This was a meeting of the Association for Parliamentary Reform, which had spread through the country. The four speakers were hostile critics of Lord North's administration, which had lost the American colonies. Sloper, whilst no doubt not wishing that the existing arrangements for returning members for Devizes be altered, would not have approved of so many rotten boroughs being in the hands of this or that politician. Devizes was not a rotten borough, even if the franchise was restricted to so few burgesses – some 20 to 30. But nothing came of the Association of Parliamentary Reform until over fifty years later. Both Whigs and Tories became nervous about extending the franchise after the French Revolution of 1789 and Sloper did not live to see the 1832 Reform Act.

In the same year, 1780, he wrote:

> Satturday Sept. 9. Generall Election when Chas. Garth Esq. and Sir James Tinly Long Baronett was unamimously Chosen Representatives for this Borough in Parliament.

Election times, both Parliamentary and Municipal, were notoriously festive, a great deal of food was eaten and alcohol consumed. Sloper and his fellow Borough voters, the burgesses, enjoyed lavish hospitality from Garth and Sir James Long. In November that year

> Chas Garth Esq. vacated his seat in Parliament on becoming appointed a Commissioner of Excise – and in consequence of which Hennry Jones Esq., a Eminent Marchant and Cloath Buyer at London, offered himself in Mr. Garth's Roome – and was elected Tuesday Nov. 28 1780.[39]

More heavy drinking took place whenever there was anything to celebrate; it was not confined to the gentry. Sloper himself kept a cellar, buying port from Garth when the latter left Devizes for London. The following year he bought from London '8 gal. of Calcavella wine for £1 15s.6d.', which included an 'Iron-bound cask'.

What may be called Sloper's 'Mayoral period' extended from his first mayoralty in 1781 to his third in 1800. A Mayor must be properly dressed and have suitable glass and crockery with which to entertain.

1781	May 12th	A new Wigg of Mr. White cost £1 1s.0d, and then paid for
	June 8th	Myself was made a magistrate and elected Mayor. New set of china £2 3s.6d.
	Sept. 3	A new wigg off Mrs. White and then paid for.

New wigs were bought annually, and in 1789 a new hat, purchased on 18 September from Robert Whitley, cost 18 shillings.

Though elected in June the Mayor did not take office until September when the Mayor took the chair at the Michaelmas charter day and kept the feast. At his election in June Sloper wrote of the church bells which rang in celebration;

June 18 1781.	To the ringers at St. John's	... £0 9s. 6d.
	To ditto at St. Mary's	... £0 7s. 6d.
	To beer to ditto 17 pints	... £0 2s. 10d.
	To green ringers	... £0 4s. 0d.

The green ringers were those at St. James, just outside the borough, generally known as the church on the green. Doubtless many healths were drunk after the formal proceedings. Entries in 1782 included:

Bear Club Feast, Fryday	Aug. 31 (an annual affair)
New Park Feast, Fryday	Sept. 20

The latter would be at the invitation of James Sutton, of New Park House, Devizes, later to sponsor his brother-in-law, the future Prime Minister Henry Addington,[40] as member for Devizes. Regular feasting was a borough way of life; on Addington's election, Sloper recorded:

1789	April 16	Election feast
	Aug 18	Sutton's feast
	Aug 20	Bear Club feast

Then before the end of September there would be a Mayor's feast.

Notwithstanding his four years as churchwarden at St. Mary's, Sloper was clearly tolerant of dissenters, particularly as far as the Reverend Robert Sloper, his nephew, was concerned, though his tolerance would probably not extend to Roman Catholics. In this he was likely to be influenced by the strongly anti-Catholic Addington. Like all local councillors, he had taken the statutory oath, 'abjuring the Pope of Rome' when he was first elected. His nephew, Robert Sloper, became a distinguished Congregationalist and a prominent member of the Countess of Huntingdon's connection,[41] the Countess founding or supporting some seventy-five dissenting chapels throughout the country. Her name appears with Robert Sloper's as trustees in the first of the Devizes Congregational chapel's title deeds.[42] Congregationalism was generally considered to be more socially acceptable than the Wesleys' Evangelism which had such an appeal to labourers and colliers. A respectable tradesman like Sloper would not be attracted by the emotional scenes often engendered by the open-air preaching of John Wesley and Rowland Hill, though he noted in 1799 – 'Monday Janye 28 – a Quaker woman from North America spoke (or preached) up in ye Town Hall in the evening'. Other substantial Devizes families, such as the Waylens, Cunningtons, Leaches and Chandlers patronised Robert Sloper's chapel, but there is no evidence that Sloper himself did.[43] He noted, certainly not with disapproval, his nephew Robert's purchase in 1802 of a considerable estate at nearby Etchilhampton for £5,590. The Reverend Sloper's wife was wealthy, which no doubt, with money inherited from his father Benjamin, enabled him to do this. Sloper approved also of his niece Anne Noyes and her family. She was Bro. Ben's daughter, and in 1798 Sloper recorded:

> Fryday Feb. 9. Putt and Bound after being one month on trial Benj Noys (for whom myself and Mr. Richd Chandler was appointed Trustees by my Brother Ben his grandfather, he being his daughter Ann's son by her husban Robt Noys) apprentice for seven years to Mr. Wm Sedgfield Grocer at ye top of The Brittox and gave £50 with him.

This was much more than the usual apprenticeship premium for a baker or grocer. However, Sloper's generosity seems to have been justified and in 1808

> Wednesday May 4 1808 – Benj Noys (son of Rob. Noys and of Ann his wife and daughter of Brother Benjn Sloper) was married in St. John's Church Devizes to Miss Sarah Smith of London and sister

> to Mrs. North wife of Mr. North mercer and draper of Devizes they are going to London and he is going to be a parttner with a person in a pretty Large Grocery way.

There seems to be satisfaction in his great-nephew young Benjamin's progress.

In his young manhood, against his record of the first year's baking in 1753, he showed a gloomy romanticism. Every month he quoted verses by James Thomson. Thus in January:

> No grass the Fields No leaves the Trees now show
> The frozen earth lyes Buried deep in Snow
> Soft Rivers are with Sudden Ice constrained
> And studdied Wheels are on its back sustained.

And February:

> The Sun from far peeps with a sickly face
> Too weak the Clouds and Mighty fogs to chase
> When up the Skyes he shoots his Rosie Head
> Or in the Ruddy Oceans seeks his Bed.

Things get better in Summer, and in August:

> Fair Summer's pride begins to fade away
> For all things there are subject to decay
> Now Ceres Golden Locks are nearly Shorn
> The Mellow Fruitt from Burdend Trees are shorn.

But in November 'stormy blasts enforce the quaking trees' and December is 'devoid of all delight'.[44] The only other verse which he transcribed, when an old man of 86, after noting the death of a faithful family servant Elizabeth Watts in 1816, was on Friendship:

> Elizabeth Watts
> Dyed March 24 1816 – Aged 75 years – having lived in this House with my Father and Mother and with Myself 60 or 61 years.
> May you be blest with all that heaven can send
> Good health, long life, good conscience and a friend.

This shows a pleasant master-servant relationship, and was an appropriate sentiment from an old gentleman. Before then, however, Sloper was to be active both as baker and as a public figure in Devizes. It is to the first of these phases of his life that we now turn.

References

1. G. M. Trevelyan, *History of England* (London, 1929), p.537.
2. J. Waylen, *A History, Military and Municipal of the Ancient Borough of the Devizes* (Devizes, 1859), p.380.
3. K. H. Rogers, *Warp and Weft* (Buckingham, 1986), p.99.
4. R. D. Gillman, *Annals of the Borough of Devizes* (Devizes, 1908), p.12.
5. *V.C.H. Wiltshire*, Vol.X, p.258.
6. H. Clarkson, *Memories of Merry Wakefield* (Wakefield, 1887), p.14.
7. *V.C.H. Wiltshire*, Vol.X, p.178.
8. J. Waylen, op. cit., p.579.
9. *Ibid.*, p.310.
10. The total is incorrect and should be £35 6s. 4d.
11. The total is incorrect and should be £18 3s. 6d.
12. *V.C.H. Wiltshire*, Vol.X, p.302.
13. C. Dale (ed.), *Wiltshire Apprentices and their Masters 1710–60*, W.A.S. Records Branch, Vol. XVII, (1961). Master bakers could command a fee of £10. In 1742 John Waylen, a baker of a well established Devizes family, asked and obtained £20, but this was exceptional. There was a fee on the articles of apprenticeship.
14. E. Bradby, *The Book of Devizes* (Buckingham, 1985), pp.44,78.
15. J. Waylen, op cit., p.413.
16. D. Mattock, 'The Wiltshire Regiment' (typescript held in W.R.O.).
17. *V.C.H. Wiltshire*, Vol.X, p.229.
18. *Wiltshire Times*, 17 Sept. 1910.
19. W.R.O. 1090/1–40, Bear Club Membership Lists; 1553/3, Bear Club Steward's Accounts.
20. *D.N.B.*, Vol.I, p.525. Aram, Eugene (1704–59) executed at York.
21. *Ibid.*, Vol.XVII, p.134. Laurence Shirley, Earl Ferrers (1720–60) hanged at Tyburn for 'in a paroxysm of passion killed his land steward'.
22. *Ibid.*, Vol.VII, p.895. Garrick, David (1717–79). The great actor was impressed by the young Lawrence at *The Bear*. Waylen, op. cit., p.448.
23. *Ibid.*, Vol.XIV, p.99. Nash, Richard (1674–1762). When 'Beau' Nash died Sloper would be 32 and becoming prosperous. Nash made nearby Bath a fashionable holiday and health centre.
24. *Ibid.*, Vol.III, p.570. Byng, Admiral John (1704–57). Contemporary prints show the unfortunate Admiral's execution by firing squad on *Monarque's* quarter deck.
25. *Ibid.*, Vol.IV, p.991. Cook, Captain James (1728–79).
26. *The Universal Magazine*, Feb. 1757.

27. *Chambers Biographical Dictionary* (1985), p.747. Flavius Josephus AD27–?100. Jewish soldier-historian. Sloper would read the translation from the Greek of which many were published in the eighteenth century.
28. W. Stukeley, *The Family Memoirs of the Rev. William Stukeley M.D.* (Surtees Society, 1884).
29. *D.N.B.*, Vol.V, p.617. Davis, James (d. 1755), Devizes Physician.
30. J. Waylen, op. cit., p.424.
31. *D.N.B.*, Vol.XV, p.1074. The correct name is Phillip Arthur (1738–1814). He was the first Governor of New South Wales.
32. *Chambers*, op.cit., p.133. Tippo Sahib was the son of Hyder Ali; both were Sultans of Mysore.
33. B. Wright, *The British Fire Marks 1680–1879* (Cambridge, 1982). The Royal Exchange Assurance was founded in 1720.
34. B. H. Cunnington, *Some Annals of the Borough of Devizes; being a Series of extracts from the Corporation Records 1535–1835* (2 Vols. 1925–26), Vol.II, p.235.
35. *D.N.B.*, Vol.XXI, p.242. Wilkes, John (1727–97). Radical politician, duellist, one of the 'infamous Monks of Medmenham', champion of the freedom of the Press, prisoner in the Tower and beloved by the City of London of which he was Lord Mayor in 1774.
36. *Chambers*, op. cit., p.577. Gordon, Lord George (1751–93). Anti-Catholic agitator. The Catholic Relief Act of 1778 influenced him to lead 50,000 protesters to the Commons, but the mob got out of hand and many Catholics' houses and chapels were burnt.
37. *D.N.B.*, Vol.V, p.210. Brass Crosby (1725–93). Was a radical Lord Mayor of London. The city and Government did not always agree.
38. *D.N.B.*, Vol.XV, p.1005. William Petty and 2nd Earl of Shelburne (1737–1805). Created Marquis of Lansdown 1784. His mansion at Bowood is 7 miles from Devizes. Prime Minister 1782–3.
39. J. Waylen, op. cit., p.406. Garth, Charles, son of John. Both M.P.s and Recorders at Devizes. Waylen gives a short history of this family.
40. *Chambers*, op. cit., p.1227; J. Waylen, op. cit., p. 546. Addington, Henry, Viscount Sidmouth (1757–1884). M.P. Devizes 1784–1805, and Recorder. The most distinguished of Devizes M.P.s.
41. *D.N.B.*, Vol.IX, p.133. Hastings, Selina, Countess of Huntingdon (1707–91). Daughter of Earl Ferrers, joined Methodists 1739, with Whitfield as her chaplain.
42. T. Broster-Temple, *St. Mary's Congregational Church* (W.A.N.H.S. pamphlet, 1962).
43. *Ibid.*
44. James Thomson, *Poetical Works* (1908). The long poem quoted by Sloper recalls the changing aspects of the seasons and the philosophic moods thereby envoked. Thomson was the author of 'Rule Britannia'.

III The Master Baker

The English people of the eighteenth century were fastidious about the quality of their bread.

Sir William Ashley, *The Bread of our Forefathers* (Oxford, 1928)

Sloper's family clearly meant a lot to him. He recorded the births, marriages and deaths of his parents, brothers and sisters, nephews and nieces. The home was a happy one. However, the allure of a pleasant home environment did not delay him from following his father into what he made a very profitable business. In 1753 he began to record his daily takings for the bread which he baked until, in 1802, '50 years wanting 6 months', as he wrote he ceased in business. He was clearly commercially successful, building up his annual takings from £173 in 1753 to a high point in 1783, when he was 53, at £3110 8s. 0d. (See Graph I).

Since the early thirteenth century the legislature had attempted by means of the Assize of Bread, to regulate the price of bread and the profit allowed to the baker.[1] The Assize's operation rested with the local magistrates – in the close borough of Devizes the Mayor of the year, the Recorder and usually before one, sometimes two, senior burgesses.[2] The original intention was to regulate the weight of a penny loaf according to the prevailing price of wheat and the grade of flour used. The clerk of the market at Devizes, a borough-appointed official, would report to the Mayor (or in practice to the Town Clerk) the average cost of a bushel of wheat sold in Devizes on a particular market day. The Corporation, which ran the market under its ancient charters, provided a 'measuring house' with scales in which the wheat, measured by the bushel, was weighed. Other commodities, such as barley, beans and flour were also weighed there. The Mayor and his magistrate colleagues then applied a recognised formula which gave the baker a theoretical profit and prescribed the obligatory weight of penny, twopenny, sixpenny and shilling loaves for the three qualities recognised – 'wheaten' – i.e. the best quality, 'household' and 'standard'.[3]

However, in 1709 an alternative system of regulating the price and weight of bread sold obtained statutory sanction, and bakers were allowed to bake to standard weights and a permitted price, this system being known as 'Priced Bread'. The Devizes magistrates adopted this method and it was operative when Sloper began his record in 1753. Ten years

Drawing of the bread stones set in the wall of the parish church of Great Wishford, Wiltshire. They record the price of a gallon loaf from 1800.

Bread making in the eighteenth Century.

Sloper's Yearly Takings and the Price of Wheat (per quarter) 1753-1801

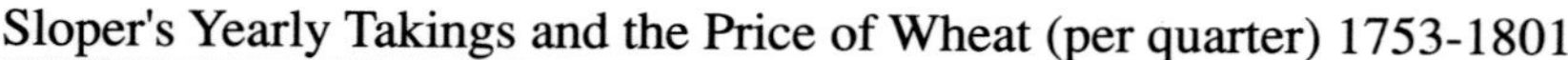

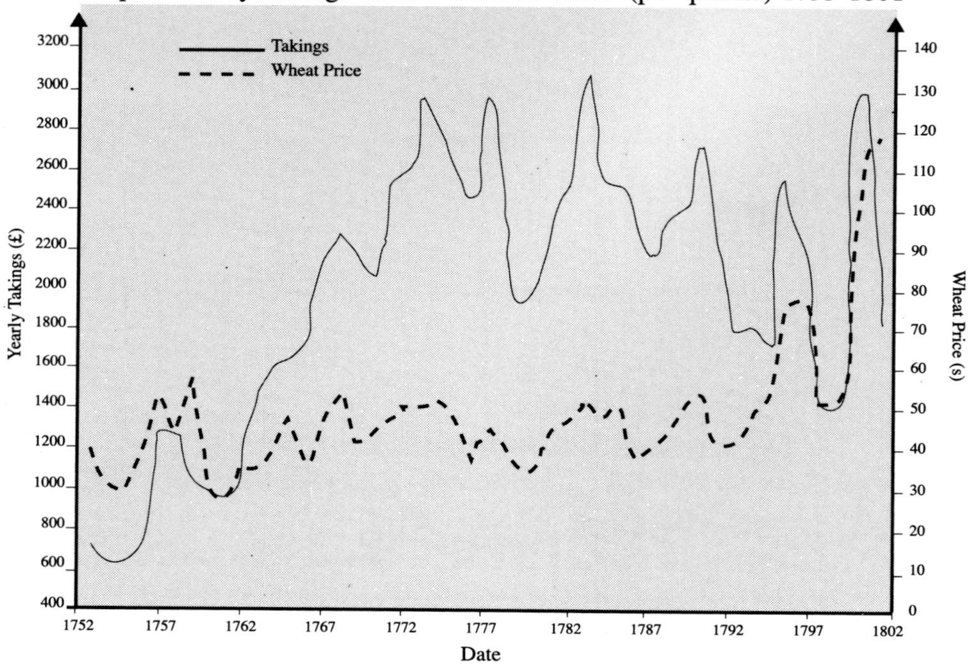
Takings
Wheat Price
Yearly Takings (£)
3200
3000
2800
2600
2400
2200
2000
1800
1600
1400
1200
1000
800
600
400
Wheat Price (s)
140
130
120
110
100
90
80
70
60
50
40
30
20
10
0
1752
1757
1762
1767
1772
1777
1782
1787
1792
1797
1802
Date

Sloper's Record of the Price of a Gallon Loaf.

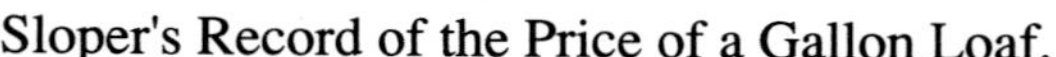

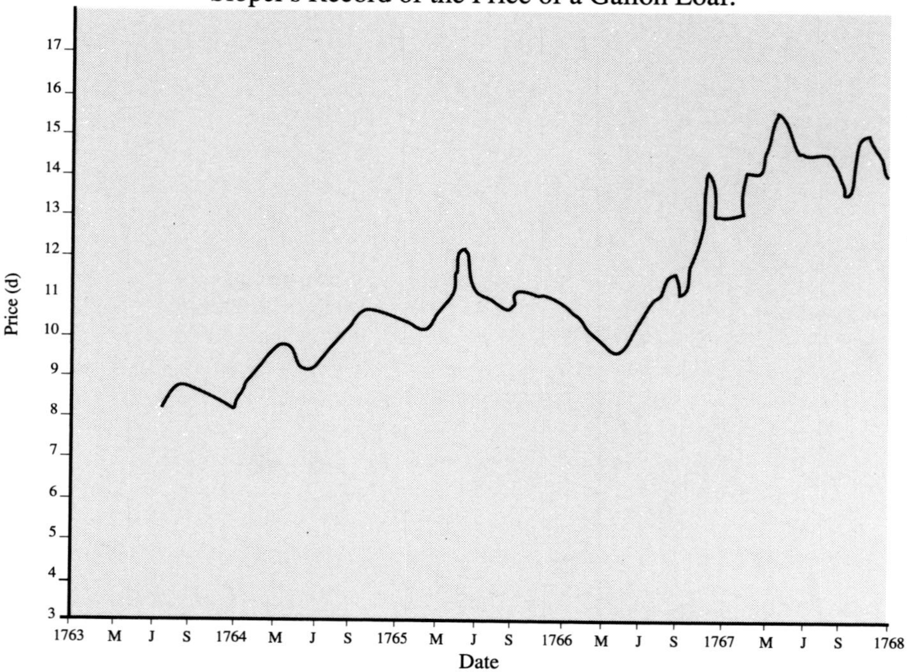
Price (d)
17
16
15
14
13
12
11
10
9
8
7
6
5
4
3
1763
M
J
S
1764
M
J
S
1765
M
J
S
1766
M
J
S
1767
M
J
S
1768
Date

later, in December 1763, when there was a wheat shortage and resultant distress and unrest, he noted 'Gallon lof 8d.', and recorded its monthly rise to 10½d. in October 1764, 1s. in the following April and 1s. 3½d., in March 1767. That November the magistrates changed their policy, reverting from fixing the price for a loaf to prescribing its weight. Sloper wrote – 'The Mayor (Mr. Flower) and Mr. Garth ye Recorder forbad the making of any more gallon or half gallon lofes in this borough from November 16 – Monday'. Both systems used the cost of wheat to decide what the price or the weight was to be.[4] Wheat price increases were sometimes attributable to war on the continent and the consequent interruption of trade, but the major cause was bad harvests. Great Britain was at war with France between 1756 and 1763, and again 1793 – 1801, and from 1802 to 1815. But not all these years were famine years. Whatever the price of wheat, Sloper continued his baking and daily record of it. The sample analysis below shows the weekly profit and clearly indicates that the more the cost price of wheat rose the more money he took. It was the ill-wind of wheat shortages which blew Sloper some good. He must have had mixed feelings and he certainly was keenly aware of fluctuating wheat prices, monitoring carefully the cost of a gallon loaf over the period from 1763 to 1767, when its baking was forbidden.

Sample Analysis Showing Sloper's Weekly Profit 1763 – 67

Week Ending	*Takings*	*Cost Price of Wheat (per quarter)*	*Loaves Baked*	*Selling Price per loaf*	*Profit**
23rd July 1763	£29 10. 0	£1 16. 1	885	8d.	£0 10. 0
7th April 1764	£34 0. 0	£2 1. 5	859	9½d.	£2 5. 0
10th November 1764	£33 0. 0	£2 1. 5	754	10½d.	£5 1. 0
27th April 1765	£36 4. 0	£2 8. 0	724	12d.	£5 14. 0
11th January 1766	£35 7. 0	£2 1. 3	809	10½d.	£5 16. 0
13th September 1766	£36 10. 0	£2. 1. 3	730	12d.	£9 15. 0
16th May 1767	£52 13. 0	£2. 7. 4	871	14½d.	£16 9. 0
29th November 1767	£44 0. 0	£2. 7. 4	754	14d.	£13 0. 0

* In addition there would be the cost of milling, yeast, salt, faggots and a journeyman paid at 7s. a week.

The selling price per loaf for the years 1763 –67 inclusive may be obtained from the Graph 1. Using the weekly takings obtained from Sloper's book the number of gallon loaves baked per week can be estimated.

Each gallon loaf, weight approximately 8 lb.
Loaves baked = Weekly Takings (pence)
÷ Selling Price (pence)

The cost of baking a gallon loaf can now be calculated. This mainly depended on the stated price of wheat shown by Graph 1. Wheat was priced per quarter (500 lbs.), which equalled 8 bushels (62½ lbs). About 60 lbs. of bread may be made per bushel of wheat, so that one bushel of wheat made approximately one bushel of bread, or eight gallon loaves. Hence a quarter of wheat made about 8 x 8 = 64 gallon loaves. Thus the cost of a gallon loaf was approximately equal to:

Price of wheat (per quarter) ÷ 64.

The profit per week is obtained by subtracting the cost price from the selling price per loaf and multiplying by the number of loaves baked.

Wages generally were very low. Sloper only paid between 4s. and 8s. per week to his journeymen bakers, and this was the general pattern for the labouring class. On these low wages the rise in the cost of their staple diet of bread in 1765 – 66, 1795 – 96 and 1801 – 02, was serious indeed, and disorder resulted in most of the midland and south-western counties. Thus on

> 14 February 1765 in Devizes
> A tumultuous mob assembled in the borough; and being armed and disguised assaulted the homes of several of the principal inhabitants, particularly those of the Mayor, the High Sheriff, the Town Clerk, the Postmaster, the Distributor of Stamps and the Excise Officers; demolishing the windows, destroying the furniture and threatening the lives of the inmates.

This riot, with disguised participants, might have been the work of smugglers, said to be well organised and really formidable at the time,[5] but it might also have been due to political feelings running high.[6]

In 1766 ' a letter from Wiltshire says the whole county are flocking to join the rioters'.[7] A mill was broken into at Bradley near Trowbridge, six miles from Devizes, the rioters dividing the corn between them. In neighbouring Berkshire, at Newbury, 'a great number of poor people assembled in the market place .... during the time of the market on account of the rise in the price of wheat when they ripped open the sacks and scattered the corn about'.[8] This was in October when in the Devizes market the price of a gallon loaf was rising from 10d. in June to 1s. 1d. in November. There was trouble at Bath and Malmesbury. At Beckington, between Bath and Devizes, 'a miller and his son got firearms to oppose the mob .... and killed a man and a boy .... which so exasperated the mob that they set fire to the mills and burnt them down'.[9] There were serious riots at Salisbury. Millers and bakers were generally targets, and Sloper must have been apprehensive. Two years later when he was 'Mayor's Constable in the Market Place', he might have found things very difficult. In 1766 a quarter of wheat cost 48s. and averaged some 50s. until 1795 when it rose steeply to 75s. 2d., and 78s. 7d. in 1796. On 12 March 1767 Sloper wrote 'Farmer Hunt of Enford sold wheat for 10 shill. a bushll. Galln. lofe 1=3'.

During the Napoleonic Wars a quarter of wheat cost as much as 119s. 6d. The Devizes authorities, Sloper among them, took what action they could. In summer 1795 the Magistrates sat weekly to review the Assize of Bread. That March Sloper resumed recording the price of a gallon loaf as he had done in the 1763 – 67 period; it was then 1s. 3d. By July it was 2s. 4d. The Magistrates appear to have lifted their ban on selling gallon loaves and Sloper recorded:

	lbs.	oz.	dws.
shill loafe	3	15	12
sixpenny	1	15	4
threepenny		15	5

the Assize of bread raised from 11/6 to 14 shill per bush that is 10 assizes in one week from July 13 to ye 20.

Presumably in that week the Magistrates sat every day and decided from the price wheat was fetching in Devizes market what the prescribed weights should be. The figure of 2s. 4d. in July was, however, the highest reached that year and the gallon loaf's cost declined to 1s. 1d. in 1797. However, as Sloper recorded, it climbed again to 2s. in November 1799 and by February 1801 it was 3s. 6d. There was a sharp fall to 1s 5d. in June 1802, probably at least partly due to the Peace of Amiens which Addington negotiated when Prime Minister. Thereafter Sloper ceased to bake . An earlier comment on the price of wheat was

A remarkable occurance

There was not one single katt-key to be found on any ash tree in the Kingdom – of the growth of (1794) last year so it was in many newspapers advertised a large premium this spring 1795 any person that could produce one single bunch of ye growth of 1794 but there was not one to be found as was ever herd of. Some people thought it an omen of the dearness of wheat this year being sold for fifteen shillings per bushell in Devizes Market.

Sloper, when Mayor in 1800, called a meeting and in response to Government proclamations issued a statement enjoining economy. In this he imitated the action of James Gent, Devizes Mayor in 1795. Only the standard wheaten bread was to be eaten, that is made from flour from which only bran has been abstracted; and a relief fund was set up in Devizes for the poor. Philanthropists took up the case of the poor, as did amateur economists like Hunt and William Cobbett. The latter was told by a hedger that he only earned 1s. 6d. a day, and there is no doubt that the poor were very poor.[10] In 1798 owing to the dangerous state of the country the burgesses decided, as Sloper noted in his record, not to hold the Mayor's Feast. Considering how they prized civic dignity and feasting this was indeed a sacrifice on the altar of national economy and patriotism. In March 1801 Sloper, as Mayor, took the chair at a Council meeting which voted £50 for the relief of the poor whose 'distresses are so much increased by the enormous price of provisions and every other necessary of life'.[11]

There can be little doubt that Sloper was a very proficient baker. His takings, improving over the years, albeit inflated during the years of wheat shortage, demonstrate this. The English people of the eighteenth century were fastidious about the quality of their bread, and by the end of the century 'wheat had become the almost universal bread-corn of the whole people, of all classes and occupations .. the attempts of well-meaning philanthropists to persuade working people to content themselves with bread of other corn .... were totally unsuccessful'.[12] To have maintained and improved his market Sloper must have made his bread from wheat-corn. Only once in his record, early in his career, did he mention any other additive, '1761 bought a sack of horse beans Monday Nov. 9th.'.[13] He may have improved the quality of his bread before that, '1754 October, the best bread baked this week'. It is a fair assumption that his bread was always of good quality. In 1762 and again in 1767 he obtained from the Corporation the contract for supplying Coventry's bread, netting him £3 1s. 0d. on the first occasion, and £5 11s. 0d. on the second. This was a bread dole to provide a loaf of bread to all households on a specific day once a year, and it probably originated in the fifteenth century when the Coventry family were prominent benefactors.[14] The tradition, unsupported by evidence according to Salmon the Town Clerk, was that a hungry and indigent wayfarer was befriended in Devizes and later, when rich, provided for the distribution of a loaf on a certain date to all in the town, including wayfarers. This could lead to ludicrous results. A travelling Austrian Archduke and his lady, happening to call at *The Bear* on the date for distribution, were solemnly presented with their loaves, an event which received notice in the *Annual Register*.[15] Sloper probably gained his contract to supply Coventry's Bread on ability and not personal influence, proper or improper, as he did not become a burgess until 1777. In 1802 it took eight men to distribute the dole and from that time it was discontinued; Sloper was Mayor at the time. The Corporation considered that their money could be better applied to a fund for the relief of the poor.

Sloper's bakehouse was an integral part of his Sheep Street house. Not unexpectedly it required periodic attention. Sloper wrote – 'in 1761 a new iron oven mouth to the great oven January 29 Thursday', a repair that lasted for 21 years. In 1765 Sloper paved the bakehouse itself and in 1770, for £5 6s. 'paved ye great oven Feb. 28. Bought a copper furnas of Farmer Lyddiard 65 lbs. at 1s. 2d'. In 1780 he paved the great oven again – '300 bricks, rubbed edges'. In 1778 he wrote 'April 6 began anew the bakehouse and it was covered in 17 days'. Doubtless he kept his oven and bakehouse in good repair. It would seem that he had both larger and smaller ovens, bricked on roof, sides and floor, with an iron door to both.[16]

Sloper doubtless rose early to bake his bread for morning sale and this involved firing the great and little ovens, kneading the dough, drawing the fire when the ovens were hot enough, and introducing the dough in fixed sizes on long-handled shovels. The work of kneading was hard, as William Cobbett observed, 'the dough must be well-worked, the fists must go heavily into it. It must be rolled over, pressed out, folded up and pressed out again .... this is labour, mind'.[17] For assistance in the bakehouse he employed a journeyman baker. In 1780 he was paying James Phillips 4s. a week, paid half yearly and in arrears (though he would willingly lend him 5 guineas). This was probably the James Phillips to whom he paid 1 guinea in 1764 to be his substitute in the unpopular militia. Phillips stayed for nine years but in 1789:

> Wait ye watchman Satt. morning Sep. 12 between 2 and 3 o'clock in ye morning saw James Phillips and his wife Hester bring several fagotts (at least 5) out of ye backside and carry them home.

Sloper forgave him but Phillips 'went away from me Dec. 5 following. He replaced him but the replacement stole 'a handkerchief of flower'.

In July 1790 Sloper 'gave Sarah Painter 10s. 6d. for ... mornings work in the bakehouse', (he does not specify the number of mornings) and on another occasion observed she 'moulds bread'. In 1791 a journeyman baker was employed at 6s. 0d. a week. By 1793 Phillips was back again (but at only 4s. a week, perhaps Sloper was not prepared to pay 6s. until he had proved himself more reliable), but again in trouble – he 'stole a great coate pocket full of flower'. Again he was forgiven and remained in Sloper's employ until at least April 1796 when he had to go to Salisbury hospital. Sloper recorded no other journeyman after that.

As well as a journeyman Sloper employed a 'bread-boy' – Richard Stephens in 1785. Stephens received 10d. a week, but in 1790 Sloper was paying only 6d. a week for bread-boy John Stretch. There were several others and these boys would live in the house. Sloper continued to employ teenage children, girls included, after he had finished baking. No doubt they were useful around the house, particularly as the faithful housekeeper Elizabeth Watts was getting older; she was over 70 in 1810. Perhaps she taught them, particularly the girls, how to bake and brew, which Cobbett was always urging on those who were to live in less affluent households,[18] and Sloper probably liked children. Certainly what evidence there is indicates a benign nature and that there is nothing of the crusty old bachelor about him.

Sloper made money. In 1770, some 17 years after he began his record, he must have accumulated capital, for he made the first of 20 property purchases, paying a modest £25 for the 'late Cleaver's house'. This was a year before his father died, when as well as inheriting the family house in Sheep Street with the bakery and business no doubt he obtained further capital by way of cash. In 1772 he was able to give £470 for a leasehold estate at Coate, a village two miles from Devizes and one mile from Neck Mill, which he had taken over in 1770. Five years later he was able to give £1,360 for the Rotherstone Estate near St. Mary's church, and he added to both the Coate and Rotherstone properties later – for example giving £1,320 for 109 acres at Coate in 1790. The total paid for his recorded property purchases is almost £7,000. These recorded property purchases are to be found in Appendix B.

His accumulation of capital must have been derived mostly from the bakery profits, but also from his rented property. In 1779, for example, part of his Coate purchase was let at £40 p.a., and in 1808 fields at Rotherstone made 40 guineas p.a.

The question arises as to how Sloper dealt with his cash before employing it, or part of it, in these property purchases. The first Devizes bank did not open until 1775, by which time he had been baking for over 20 years and made the two substantial Coate and Rotherstone purchases mentioned. Before banks were formally instituted the clothiers in a textile district requiring capital would borrow cash from those in their locality looking for an outlet for their money.[19] It is very probable that the Suttons at New Park or Town End, or both, would take Sloper's money, perhaps at 5%; as his record carefully notes, in 1755, that under a statute of Queen Anne this was the standard rate. He was very well acquainted with the Suttons and he recorded a loan to James Sutton, though not of his own money, of £250 in 1785:

> Recd. Nov. 4 1785 of James Sutton of New Park Esq., a Note of Hand for two hundred and fifty pounds being the Property and Capitall Stock of the Gardners Club of Devizes (to carry interest at £5 p. cent p. annum from July 9 last.) Which said Note of Hand I saw putt in the Club Box at the Black Horse the evening of the day and date above written.
> The above note bears the date July 9 1789.

Sloper had money of his own to lend, thus in 1804 a carter 'had £80 in my hands' on his death by suicide, and he supplied bread on credit. 'Widdow Ellen' had loaves delivered for over four years from 1783, and her friend or relative settled with Sloper on a six monthly basis. When he died in 1821 he was by local standards a rich man. An estimate of his total capital could well place it at £10,000 or more because to the value of his recorded purchases must be added the Sheep Street house, and cash on loan or at the bank. Indeed he may well by the time he 'gave off bakin' have been amongst the most wealthy of the tradesmen of Devizes, though he was considerably less wealthy than his corporation colleague Samuel Adlam, of whom he wrote:

> He died suddenly May 12 1811. His property was supposed to be not less than £40,000 in the 79th year of his age.

Sloper would not be as well-off as Wadham Locke II of Rowde Ford, Solicitor and Banker, or as Salmon the Town Clerk, and he was certainly a long way behind the two branches of the clothier's family of Sutton at New Park and Town End. The New Park branch had, by the end of Sloper's life, firmly established themselves amongst the gentry, and the Town End branch had become bankers.

On the last page of Sloper's record of 'baked bread', of family notes of births, marriages and deaths, and of national and borough municipal affairs he wrote, aged 72;

> Memorandum that there was baked in bread from Jan 1 1753 to June 29 1802 being 50 years wanting 6 months £98,446 being average about £1,969 p.a.

And he added;

> Gave off bakin Tuesday June 29 1802
> Ended baking Tuesday June 29 1802.

Perhaps what is more remarkable than the quantity of bread baked – nearly £100,000 worth – is the consistency with which the daily takings are noted. Barring a few Thursdays until 1757, an occasional fast day, and of course all Sundays, Sloper baked every day and noted the money he took – for six days a week, 313 days a year, for, as he says, 50 years.

Sloper is silent on how he sold his bread. He certainly found customers amongst the shopkeepers. Thus in 1766, a year of shortage, he wrote 'Jan. 13 Monday agreed by all the bakers of Devizes to serve no shops with gallon lofes'. (The regulated price was 10d. and rising.) Whilst the more prosperous families doubtless baked their own bread the average citizen, poorly paid with bread prices rising and little prospect of an increase in earning capacity, would buy his bread from the local shops. Sloper does not indicate that he had a shop himself, nor do contemporary gazetteers state that he had. However, when he ultimately sold his business in 1802 he may well have passed on the goodwill of the name of 'George Sloper' to his successor. Certainly someone was trading as a baker under that name in the Brittox, the main street where one would expect to find the best quality shops, in 1830 – nine years after Sloper's death. The probability is therefore that Sloper had a shop in the Brittox as his main outlet as well as, no doubt, the bakehouse itself.

It is practically certain that he also had a bread round. He recorded that he sold bread at Stert (where he had a small mill), 2 miles from Devizes, and he could well have sold bread in other villages as well. For this he would require a van, horses and someone to drive. He recorded purchases of a van or cart:

To a new cart in October 1774	
To sundry viz.	6 10. 10
To ... iron axels and other iron belong to ye cart	
To ... wheels for the cart	4 12. 6
To Gamble for writing name	1. 6
To Wm. Bishop for painting	12. 0
To iron boxes to date	1. 4

Sloper "gave off baking June 29 1802". The general thanksgiving to which he refers is the Peace of Amiens. Addington had succeeded Pitt as Prime Minister and the re-election of the former for Devizes is noted.

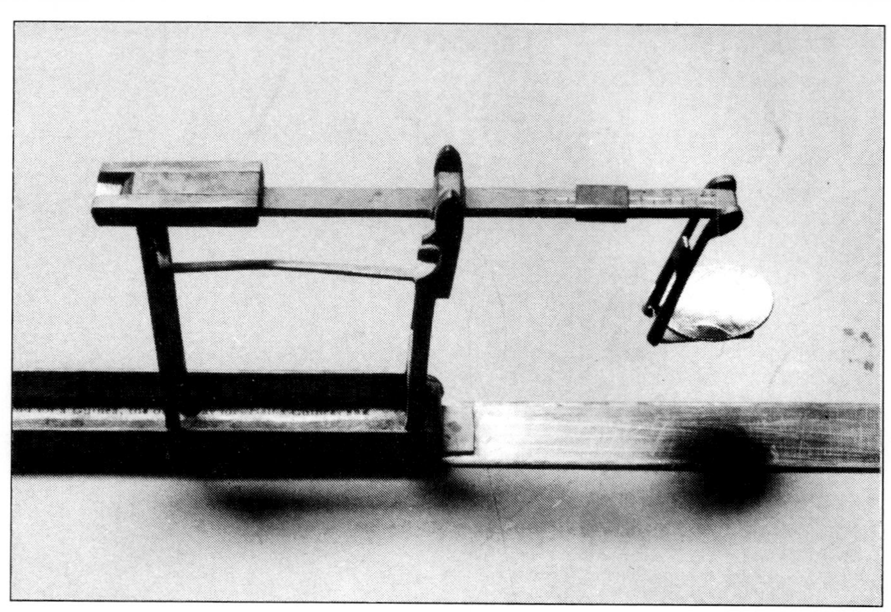

George Sloper's scales, used to check that the weight of gold in the guinea and half guinea corresponded with its nominal value, 5 pennyweight or 2 pennyweight. This was a precaution against clipping the edges.

Examples of 18th century guineas.

What the iron boxes were for is not apparent – possibly for keeping the bread warm during delivery. The cart would no doubt also be used to transport the flour from his mill to the bakehouse. In 1785 he bought a 'new little cart' – again with boxes and with a 'tail and red ladder and sideboards'. The word 'little' would indicate that he had a larger one and that the business was prospering, necessitating two vehicles for delivery and use in connection with his mill. The improved figures for his takings bear this out.

Sloper only recorded two instances when be bought horses, cobs, paying 15 guineas on each occasion, but the entries are partly illegible and detail absent. No doubt either Sloper or his journeyman baker and perhaps his bread-boy drove the carts.

Besides baking Sloper had another commercial activity – that of milling, which he carried on at Neck Mill, Stert, a small village two miles from Devizes. As early as 1737 his father occupied this mill in partnership with one John Rose, and Sloper first took it over in 1770, having been, he records, 'kept out of it about 19 years', which would indicate that he had expectations to run it from 1751 when he was 21 years old. His legal interest in it as tenant, sub-tenant, copyholder or freeholder, is not clear. Most of the village of Stert, including two mills, was owned by New College, Oxford, but the college archives disclose no Sloper or Rose as tenant although it is possible that Neck Mill may be listed under Coate parish.[20] The most likely explanation is that Sloper's father, Rose and Sloper himself were sub-tenants of a tenant of the College holding by the common device of a lease for three lives – those of Sloper's father, Rose and Sloper himself. Sloper used this legal device when a copyholder of the Manor of Bishops Cannings – the three lives being his own, his nephew the Reverend Robert and Robert's son Samuel.

It was pointed out at the time how financially advantageous it was to make your own flour instead of buying it:

> after it has passed through the hands of a corn merchant, a miller, a flour merchant and a huxter, every one of whom does and must have a profit out of the flour.[21]

Sloper would buy his corn locally, either at the Devizes weekly market or perhaps direct from the nearby farms, was his own miller and needed no flour merchant or huxter. This milling must have been profitable but as no records survived it is impossible to elaborate. Though the mill was small with one pair of stones only, the volume of flour it produced warranted both a journeyman and a loader. Besides grinding for Sloper's bakehouse it probably ground for external sales. When he took it over in 1770 his takings increased by nearly 50% in three years and this was doubtless partly due to Sloper the baker obtaining his flour at a cheaper rate than previously. The mill, which had an overshot wheel, exists no longer, though the mill pond can still be seen and is fed by a stream running down the valley on the west of Etchilhampton Hill. In 1771 Sloper recorded than he stocked the pond with 20 brace of tench and 4 brace of carp, presumably for the benefit of his larder. Sloper's miller for 32 years was Robert Offer, and when the latter retired in 1802 Sloper replaced him by Stephen Acorman at 10s. a week, who stayed for eight years at least, by which time Sloper was no longer keeping his record. The mill machinery required attention from time to time. In 1776 Sloper noted, 'June 18. Began pulling down at mill the water wheel and trunk and shaft, in order to rebuild it'. It took five weeks to do these repairs. Three years later the shroud boards and wheel buckets needed attention. In 1781 Sloper provided 'a new wire flour and dressing machine at Nick Mill May 4.'. This would be for bolting the flour by sieving it to remove the bran and make it suitable for 'best quality wheaten' bread. The fact that Sloper ground flour at this mill for at least 40 years, and that he kept milling after he ceased baking must mean that Neck Mill was a source of substantial profit, even when he was no longer grinding for himself.

Sloper saved money by his own brewing. When he was a boy nearly all households in the country, cottagers included, brewed for themselves. In the 1820s it was said:

> In former times, to set about to show to Englishmen that it was good for them to brew beer in their houses would have been .... impertinent .... only 40 years ago to have a house and not to brew was a very rare thing indeed.[22]

Sloper first recorded his brewing in 1781, but it would be surprising if he were not brewing earlier having learnt the art from his parents. In that year he wrote:

> Brewed March 26 8 gal of best No. 6
> 2 Powells
> 10 Powells No. 3 beer and ale No. 8

In 1782 he wrote:

> Washed No. 6 Nov. 4 and 5
> Brewed Nov. 19 – 12 bushell Adlam and filled Old Tom
> Nov. 26 – Danl. Neet No. 5

His recordings are intermittent but it is clear that he brewed at least on two days twice a year – usually in February or March, and in November. Thus:

1795 Feb. 7 Brewed 12 Powells Old Tom
12 Powells 5
12 Waylen 3 Ale

Amongst his last brewing entries are '1805 Dec. 6. Taped No. 6' and

1807 Feb. 11 Brewed 10 Bush Malt
Mr. James Gent No. 6 best.
Feb. 12 Brewed 10 of Mr. James Gent
No. 1 and 13 and brewed 10 of Mr. Heywood of Roundway best and second.

The bushels are bushels of malt. According to Cobbett one bushel of malt made 18 gallons of beer.

Taking the brewing of 11 and 12 Feb. 1807 as an example, James Gent the maltster sold Sloper 20 bushels, and he brewed sufficient beer to fill casks No. 6, 1 and 13. Heywood sold him 10 bushels. In total, therefore he made 450 gallons (4,230 pints) of beer to last for 6 months. This was a consumption of approximately 24 pints a day – not excessive for his household, journeyman (baking was hot work), and no doubt his visitors. The Powells, Waylens, Adlams, Neates and Gents, from whom Sloper bought his malt, were all well-established families in the town. Samuel Adlam was a clothier turned maltster, and James Gent primarily a brewer. They or members of their families were all members of the Corporation, and Sloper would rub shoulders with them on a basis of equality. He had at least 16 casks and often refers to 'Old Tom' – presumably a hogshead. He left no complete annual list of his brewing as he did for his baking, but an incomplete one for 1774 to 1789 indicates that he was buying between 33 and 74 bushels of malt per annum, with an exceptional high point in 1775 of 104 bushels, and a low one of 22 bushels in 1778. He was meticulous over the cleanliness of his casks before he filled them, with many references such as 'washed No. 6'. He made cider as well as beer. One of the two entries on this reads '1794 Oct. 8. Made a hogshead of cyder from Mill apples', and on 16 October 1801 he made 80 gallons of cider and 25 gallons of a liquor which cannot be identified from his diary.

Sloper was brewing when he was 80. In 1799 he recorded that the Parish Clerk of Stert had bought his bread for 40 years. To have given satisfaction for so long to a customer is perhaps a fitting tribute to George Sloper, Master Baker. He seems to have kept his friends as he did his customers.

References

1. E. David, *English Bread and Yeast Cookery* (London, 1977), p.226.
2. B. H. Cunnington, *Some Annals of the Borough of Devizes; being a Series of Extracts from the Corporation Records 1535 – 1835* (2 Vols. 1925–26), II, pp.208, 223.
3. *Ibid.*, I, p.xii.
4. E. David, op. cit., p.229.
5. J. Waylen, *A History, Military and Municipal of the Ancient Borough of the Devizes* (1859), p.406.
6. *Ibid.*, p.546
7. *The Gentleman's Magazine*, Vol.XXXVI (1766), p.437.
8. *Ibid.*, p.388.
9. *Ibid.*, p.437.
10. W. Cobbett – *Cottage Economy*, Essay No. 1 (London, 1836).
11. B. H. Cunnington, op. cit., II, p.13.
12. Sir William Ashley, *The Bread of our Forefathers* (Oxford, 1928).
13. J. Pennington. 'Things Unseen and Forgotten' (unpublished Portsmouth Polytechnic Diploma in English Local History dissertation, 1983). Horse beans are the modern broad beans.
14. *V.C.H. Wiltshire*, Vol.X, p.308; B. H. Cunnington, op. cit., II, p.14.
15. *Annual Registe*r, Sept. 25th 1786.
16. E. David, op. cit., p.155.
17. W. Cobbett, op. cit., Essay No. 4.
18. *Ibid.*, Essay No. 3.
19. H. Clarkson, *Memories of Merry Wakefield* (Wakefield, 1887), p.49. The failure of a merchant house in the textile trade could ruin many small investors.
20. Information from Caroline Dalton, Assistant Archivist, New College, Oxford, March 1988.
21. W. Cobbett, op. cit., Essay No. 3.
22. *Ibid.*, Essay No. 1.

IV The Public Man

Now tell I, Jarge, what thee did zee
when thee went in to Vizes town.
Did ee zee the Mayer in's royle red robe
And the Carperations standin roun?

Stephen Reynolds, *Official Guide of the Devizes Corporation* (Bournemouth 1906)

Sloper's entry into public life came with his appointment at Easter at the age of 32 as Overseer of the Poor for his parish of St. Mary's in 1762.[1] This was an office likely to be onerous owing to the declining textile trade, wheat shortages following poor harvests and the resultant number of mouths to be fed at parish expense. Sloper's duty was to raise a rate to meet the bare necessities of the needy, food, clothing, occasional boarding, apprenticing and small cash grants. His work was subject to the scrutiny of the parishioners, or such of them as attended vestry meetings. He was also asked by the wealthy clothier James Sutton, to assist in the distribution of £1000 under Thomas Thurman's will to the poor of St. Mary's – 'more than 1500 of them' – a sad reflection on the country's economic state.[2] Then in 1775 he wrote – 'chosen churchwarden by ye Minister second time April 8'. Further evidence of his popularity is that the new rector as is customary 'beat the bounds' by perambulating around the town, and so recorded Sloper – 'May 25 Wednesday I gave them cake and ale over pales at the end of the garden.'

In 1777 he became a Borough Chamberlain – one of two – responsible for its finances, and a meticulously kept record of receipts and payments survives.[3] He wrote with particular pleasure:

> Memorandum – my father Sam Sloper chosen in the Common Council Dec. 4 1727. Whitt. .... Mr. Richard Read, Mr. Thos. Whitfield elected Magistrates. Mr. Reed elected Mayor. Matthew Figgins, George Sloper, Stephen Hillman, Matthew Gent, Rbt. Bruges chosen Common Councell. Monday May 23.
> Oct. 3 – I was chosen and sworn in Chamerlain with Mr. Whitfield.

It is probable that some great matter of borough business was responsible for the following entry:

> 1778. Went to London with Mr. Matthew Gent and Mr. Salmon. Monday morn Feb. 9 at 4 clock and arrived at London 5 clock the same evening. Came home to Devizes Sunday evening February 15.

Gent was the second Chamberlain and Salmon the Town Clerk.

The Council which Sloper joined was an oligarchy of the more prosperous citizens of the borough of Devizes. As Burgesses they drew their authority from charters dating from the 13th century, the latest being that of James II in 1688. They elected whom they chose, and then they chose from amongst their friends, keeping their total number small – some 60 early in the 18th century but reducing to less than 30 at the end of it.[4] In the opinion of local government historians close corporations governed little, in essence they were undemocratic, archaic survivals kept alive only by their privilege of returning Members of Parliament.[5]

To quote a summary in the Encyclopaedia Britannica:

> 'The Corporation ... became irresponsibly close bodied regarding the borough revenues as their own property and themselves practically as clubs .... the material and social needs .... of the 18th century had to be supplied by other agencies, both statutory and voluntary. The advance of non-conformity further emphasised the unrepresentative character of the Corporations. By 1830 with some notable exceptions they were strongholds of corrupt or bigoted obscurantism in the midst of a country transformed by industrial development and alive with new political economic and social movements.'[6]

If we apply these somewhat harsh judgements to the Borough of Devizes it is certainly true that the full rights of a burgess were not enjoyed by all the inhabitants and that the freedom was closely guarded. In Sloper's time the Corporation consisted only of the Mayor, Recorder and three separate classes of burgesses – known as Capital Burgesses of the Common Council, Burgesses of the Common Council and Free Burgesses – a total fluctuating between 20 and 30. But it would be unfair to say that they treated borough revenues as their own property, there being no evidence to show that they personally bought or leased corporation property on other than open market terms. As to being a club, they certainly feasted together on such occasions as mayoral and parliamentary elections and national thanksgiving, using borough income to supplement what they personally contributed to the cost, but as they had no power to raise a rate on the inhabitants that cost did not fall on the latter. Furthermore, because they had no rating power they were quite unable to meet contemporary material and social needs. Improving the borough's streets was, for this reason, left to Improvement Commissioners (all burgesses and some 60 or more being appointed Commissioners).[7] To its credit the Corporation encouraged education, appointing a schoolmaster and providing a school. It had funds specifically for educational purposes,[8] for almshouses and for poor relief.[9] Furthermore, there is no evidence that it misapplied these funds. As to the 'advance of non-conformity' if the Devizes burgesses never elected a non-conformist in the first years of George III, by the end of his reign they were accepting Quakers.[10] Tolerance was growing.

The minutes of the Council meeting at which Sloper was admitted as burgess in 1777 survive, very neatly written by William Salmon, the very influential Town Clerk. There were present William Read, the Mayor, Charles Garth, the Recorder, and six of the seven other Capital Burgesses of the Common Council, the absentee being snuff-maker William Leach. Of a possible 13 burgesses of the Common Council 10 were present, including Sloper's brother Richard, one absentee being Robert Noyes, Sloper's nephew by marriage. Neither of the two Free Burgesses was present. The first recorded business was the unanimous elevation of Richard Read and Thomas Whitfield from Burgess of the Common Council to Capital Burgess Councillor. Then, as Sloper records, he and four others were made Free Burgesses 'and came and were severally sworn', after which they were immediately made Burgesses of the Common Council. Then, the Minutes record, 'The Act of Parliament against bribery and corruption in the election of members to serve in Parliament was publicly read'.[11] This meeting being on the Charter Day in May was the one where the Mayor for the ensuing year was chosen, to take office at Michaelmas. The names put forward were those of Richard Read, Thomas Whitfield and James Sutton Snr. The putting forward of more than one name was a formality as the outgoing Mayor proposed Richard Read and the vote was unanimous.

As Chamberlain, Sloper was responsible for at least part of the borough finances. The accounts of his stewardship survive, as clearly written by Salmon as were the borough minutes.[12] The part which Thomas Whitfield, Sloper's colleague, played as Chamberlain is unknown for the accounts are in Sloper's sole name. He was Chamberlain for four years, from his appointment for the year 1777 – 78 until his first mayoralty in

1781. Salmon did not, however, prepare the accounts until 1784, Sloper then commenting somewhat acidly:

> Gave up my 4 year Chamberlain accs. for ye years 1778, 1779, 1780, 1781 May 1784. I should give up the above accs. long before butt Mr. Salmon was engaged and he neglected calling a committy from time to time.

Sloper's Chamberlain accounts show for the four years a turnover of £917, with receipts from rents of the Wool Hall, Corn Market and Meat Shambles, fines on granting and renewal of leases, and for failure to attend Council meetings or accept office, and quit rents. The appointment of Chamberlain was an annual one, and he must have given satisfaction to his burgess colleagues to be re-elected for four years running; he served a further four years as Chamberlain in the 1790s. In the 1780s the post was usually a preliminary to becoming Mayor and seems to have been not particularly popular later, Salmon eventually holding it himself as well as being Town Clerk.

Early in 1781 Sloper would know that it was likely that he would become Mayor that year. Of the 10 Capital Burgesses of the Common Council from whom Mayors were customarily chosen, all had held the office previously, several more than once. He was a substantial property owner, and seems to have been personally respected and popular. The previous year at the Borough Quarter Sessions the Grand Jury, formed by invitation of the current Mayor from the more responsible citizens, had chosen him as its Foreman. His business was prospering – his annual takings from 'bread baked' had increased from £617 in 1754 to over £3,000 by 1780. Possibly because as Mayor he would have a lot of official business to conduct from his house, he made substantial alterations to it – a new kitchen, stables and garden wall, for example, and bought a 'new sett of china £2.12.6' and a 'new marble chimnie at £6.14.9.'. Of course he had to be appropriately dressed, gowns were obligatory for Mayors and Capital Burgesses of the Common Council, and he would have one; proper Mayoral head-dress was needed – 'May 12 – New Wigg of Mr. White and then paid for'. These last three words may well be one clue to Sloper's commercial prosperity – nothing obtained on credit, though he would give generous credit himself on occasions.

There are few other references in the diary regarding his apparel. Certainly later in life he noted that he bought hats and, on one occasion, a hat-box. The hats were no doubt of the tricorn variety, suitable for mayoral occasions. He also, latterly, wore the wig in accordance with contemporary custom for respectable citizens and had his wigs dressed, that is powdered. He recorded in 1804:

> Mem. June 23. Bought a New Coate and Breeches
> of Samll Slade (Calld) Spanish Cloath Dark Couler
> 3 yards at 10s - - - £2.17s.0d.
> To do for making
> To Mr. Williams for Trimming for ditto

Probably the nearest illustration of contemporary male dress in Devizes can be obtained from a print of the Market Place in 1760 – tricorn hats, breeches to the knee and white stockings are clearly visible.

In accordance with long-standing Devizes custom the ceremony of mayor-making was in two parts. On the Charter Day of the Friday in Whitsun week which in 1781, the year of Sloper's first mayoralty, fell on June 8 he wrote, 'myself was made a Magistrate and elected Mayor'. But he did not take up the office, again according to custom, until the Charter Day of September 29 when 'myself sworn as Mayor'. Before actually occupying the Mayoral chair he had to take the statutory Oaths of Allegiance and Supremacy. The wording of the Oaths was explicit, for instance, Sloper would

> Truly and sincerely testify and declare .... before God and the world that our Sovereign Lord King George is lawful and rightful King of this Realm .. and that not any of the descendants of the person who pretended to be Prince of Wales during the life of the late King James II .... had any right or claim whatever to the Crown of this Realm.[13]

The gentry and borough burgesses throughout the country were well satisfied with the accord between King and Parliament, and although the Allegiance Oath remained, the Stuart cause was long dead before Sloper became Mayor of Devizes for the first time in 1781.

But if no gentry or burgess now feared a return of the Stuart rule, they disliked very strongly indeed any revival in Roman Catholicism, partly because they had grown used to their Anglican Church, the clergy ranks of which they filled from their own class, and partly because Catholic France and Spain were England's traditional enemies. The most notable of the Borough's members, Addington, was a leading exponent of this thinking. Hence the Oath of Supremacy when Sloper swore that he did

> From my heart abhor, detest and abjure as impious

> and heretical that damnable doctorine ... that Princes .... excommunicated by the Pope .... of Rome may be .... murdered by their subjects .... and no foreign prince prelate or potentate have .... any jurisdiction ecclesiastical or spiritual, within this Realm.

At Sloper's installation as Mayor on Michaelmas Day other Officers were also elected, the Chamberlains, the Sergeants at Mace (who carried the maces on formal occasions), the Beadle, Clerk of the Markets and Ale Taster, the Searchers of Leather, the Searchers of Fish and Flesh, and the Market Bellman. The formalities over, the occasion was celebrated and concluded by what the Borough records describe as the Mayor's 'entertainment', the major cost of which fell on the Mayor himself. Many toasts would be drunk – the King, the Constitution, the Mayor, the late Mayor, the Members of Parliament for the Borough, the Recorder and doubtless many more.[14] As each toast was proposed, and a response made, the 'entertainment' would take many hours.

Sloper would be accustomed to these feasts, as he often refers to them. There was always one at election time given by the successful candidates, who also entertained the constituency burgesses on other occasions. Thus between Sloper's election as Mayor in June and taking office at Michaelmas, his record discloses:

> Sept. 19: Went with the Corporation to Sir James Longs, at Draycott.
>
> Sept. 21: Friday dined at Mr. Sutton's at New Park with the Corporation.

and on

> Christmas Day: (by which time he was Mayor) Sir James Tynley Long and James Sutton of New Park Esq. dined with me.

The first official legal business which Sloper records in performing as a Magistrate was on 2 January 1782, when Salmon, the Town Clerk, brought before him his 'serving boy' alleging that he had stolen 2s. The lad seems to have admitted it and Sloper committed him to the Bridewell to await Borough Quarter Sessions on the 18th. There he was found guilty, though his punishment is unrecorded. Sloper as Mayor, had chosen the Grand Jury, and his older brother Ben was its Foreman.

Sloper's work as a Magistrate was set against a somewhat difficult background. G. M. Trevelyan has written,

> To deal with the ill-sorted masses of humanity huddled together in the towns, there was no better police than the old Watchman with his rattle and the police magistrate Fielding's Bow Street Runners, fit but few. As late as 1780 the Lord George Gordon mob fairly set fire to London before the troops were called out. Mounted highwaymen beset the roads converging upon London with scandalous impunity, and were popularly regarded as the representatives of careless English valour and freedom.[15]

Applying this summary of 18th century 'law and order' to Devizes we can see that the Borough Council supplied the watchman. It must, however, have been unusual for the blind Magistrate, Sir John Fielding, to leave his Bow Street Court for a small provincial town like Devizes. Sloper noted in 1768, 'Nov. 25 Nesbitt and Wilson examined before Sir John Fielding at *The Bear* for forgery and committed to Bridewell'.[16] Sloper often noted the decisions of, and penalties ordered, by the Courts, particularly those of the Lent and Summer Assizes held at Salisbury, for instance:

> 1764 Aug. 14 Tuesday. Wm. Jaques hanged in chains this day at Stanton near Chippenham, for killing a black man near the same place.

After the Spring Assize in 1773 there was another hanging in chains (for a murder near Pewsey) and in 1801, a year of acute economic distress, 'seven men hanged at Salisbury for divers offences viz. robbery, sheep stealing, horse stealing etc.'.

Sloper reported several cases of highway robbery – for example in April 1770 a hanging in chains for robbing the mail at Beckhampton Down. Two men were 'tried and condemned' at the Lent Assizes of 1784 for robberies on the Devizes to Potterne Road (though they only collected 'five shillings and some half-pence and 18/6'). The death sentence was commuted to transportation to America for seven years (Botany Bay was not then established). In 1786 a cheesemonger was, reported Sloper, 'somehow aquited' for highway robbery at Wedhampton, and in 1790 there was another highway robbery in Bedboro Lane, Devizes on a dark November night. But he was not simply concerned with law and order.

On 28 September 1781 Sloper wrote, having just become Mayor, 'the lamps having first lighted'. This refers to the lighting of the streets by oil lamps on oak posts 10 feet high, or fixed to wall brackets, some 90 of them throughout the town. This was the work of the Devizes Improvement Commissioners. They formed a statutory body created in

1780 by an 'Act for amending regulating cleansing lighting watching and keeping in repair the streets, lanes and passages within the borough of Devizes and for preventing of nuisances ....,' of which latter there must have been many and extremely noisome, as there were no town drains and no organised refuse collection.[17] Sloper attended the early meetings of the Commissioners as one of their number and as Mayor Elect, and later as Mayor and Chairman. Rates of 9d. in the pound were levied, scavengers and night watchmen appointed and lamps erected. One lamp was well placed, no doubt Sloper thought, at the top of Morris Lane opposite his house.

Between his first mayoralty in 1781 and his second ten years later in 1791 Sloper recorded various events on the national and international scene, as well as those he considered interesting as local matters, and those in municipal affairs. Thus when there was a general election:

> 1784 April 5. Sir James Long and Henry Addington Esq. chosen mem. Parliament for the Borrough. James Lubbock of London Esq. declining standing the Pole for the sake of peace.

No doubt Lubbock concluded that he would not get a majority of the 25 odd votes of the burgesses – which with so small an electorate would not have been difficult to forecast. And as was customary after each parliamentary election, 'Election Feast April 16'.

This election brought William Pitt to full power. Long and Addington, both staunch Tories, would support Pitt. Sloper wrote,

> Right Honourable Wm. Pitt Esq. now First Lord of the Treasury and Chancellor of the Exchequer (and sone of the Right Hon. Wm. Pitt Esq.) was born in June 1759. His father was Secretary of State.

In 1789, the year of the French Revolution, Sloper wrote:

> Feb. 3 Tuesday. Mr. Francis Bailey Mayor – an addres of thanks was unanimously agreed on at a Court of Common Council to be presented to the Right Honourable Wm. Pitt Chancellor of the Exchequer for his upright and good conduct as Prime Minister at this critical time to be presented to him by our two representatives in Parliament Henry Addington and Joshua Smith Esq.

The Perpendicular nave of the Church of St. Mary with the Norman arch and chancel at the far end.

Gentlemen of the Devizes Loyal Volunteers, September 18th 1799.
Sloper said "The coulers were presented by Miss Sutton and Mrs Addington".

No doubt the Devizes burgesses were proud of those whom they sent to Parliament. The following must have given particular cause for pride and pleasure: Sloper wrote on 8 June 1789:

> Henry Addington Esq. chosen Speaker of the House of Commons and approved by the King the next day Tuesday 9th June in the House of Lords on which occasion Mr. Addington addressed the King in an elegant and pertiant speech.

The unfortunate George III had just recovered from a period of mental illness and in September 'came through Devizes from Weymouth and Longleat in his road to Windsor. He changed horses at ye *Bear* but did not get out of his coach.' The Mayor and Corporation, no doubt Sloper amongst them, attended at *The Bear*. The King's recovery was marked by 'dinner and rejoicing at ye Town Hall'.

Sloper's second mayoralty, in 1791 –2, did not result in many entries in his record, and as usual he interspersed major international events with local ones. Thus:

> June 7. Myself elected Mayor ye second time.
> June 21. The King and Queen of France ran away.
> Sept. 29. Myself was sworn in Mayor.

The Quarter Sessions in January 1792 seem to have dealt with one case, of theft of a tea chest, but the thief was in a poor state of health so only received six days in the Bridewell. On 29 March Sloper committed a young man to Salisbury Assizes for theft of silver spoons. A more interesting activity must have been calling on 19 March 'at the request of several respectable inhabitants' a public meeting 'to consider the propriety of petitioning Parliament for the abolition of the slave trade'. This motion was duly carried.

Salmon's minutes of the work of the Corporation extend what Sloper recorded, for example just before Michaelmas Day, when he was due to be sworn in as Mayor, he is recommended to hold his 'entertainment' on the Friday, the day after market day (probably because full justice would not be done to the enjoyment of the 'entertainment' if burgesses had a lot of market business to conduct). Again, on 21 November, Sloper presiding, Salmon minuted some four pages of recorded leases, mostly for 99 years, with fines to the Corporation, that is payments on a granting or renewal of a lease additional to the annual quit rent, and market tolls let for seven years at £101 17s. 0d. p.a. It must have pleased Sloper when in May 1792 Joshua Smith M.P., followed the custom of the borough Member subsidising the Corporation by promising £500 for Borough Funds. Then on 11 June Sloper as Mayor signed a Loyal Address to the Crown, clearly inspired by the fear caused by the French Revolution.[18]

In 1800 Sloper served as Mayor for the third and last time. It was a very worrying period; at home the price of wheat was soaring while the fears of the gentry and bourgeoisie following the terror engendered by the French Revolution, coupled with the war with France, were very real. Perhaps for these reasons Sloper's journal entries are short:

> June 1. I was elected Mayor being the third time.
> June 12. Farmer Gibbs sold wheat for one guinea per bushell .... in Devizes Market.
> Oct. 24. Gallon lofe standard 3/-

He did not mention his inauguration as Mayor on Michaelmas Day, but 'Sept. 13 a new wigg .... and paid for the same'. However, he had the somewhat unusual duty as Mayor and Returning Officer of presiding in one year at two by-elections. On 25 February 1801 Addington accepted Cabinet office and this meant he had to submit himself again to his constituents, the burgesses of the close borough of Devizes. Similarly when he became Prime Minister there had to be an election on 21 March and he was re-elected on each occasion without opposition. Another duty involved presiding at the borough's Petty Sessions for example when butter was being sold in the market 'four ounces short of weight in one pound as it weighed only 12 oz.'. He confiscated the dealer's stock and 'the whole the person had I gave to the poor people'. Others were caught too selling 'short weight' amounting in all to 29 lbs., from which the poor benefited, and he fined a baker 10s. for selling a 'half-pecke loafe short of weight 15 oz.'.

By 1800 Sloper was 70, well-known in Devizes, and knowledgeable on its affairs and citizens. While he doubtless knew the Sutton family of New Park well by report, he is unlikely to have known the then head of the family, James Sutton III, personally until he became a burgess in 1777, when invitations to dine would be exchanged between the Mayor, Richard Read, and the two members of Parliament. Sloper describes these dinners as feasts. The Suttons were established in Devizes in the 1690s, and had gone from strength to strength. In 1771 James Sutton III, M.P. for Devizes since 1765, married Eleanor Addington, daughter of Prime Minister William Pitt's Physician, and sister of Henry Addington, later Viscount Sidmouth. James Sutton III and Eleanor Addington had two sons who died in infancy, and two daughters. Sloper recorded the deaths

Devizes Market Place c 1798 showing the old Market Cross
and the pillar-mounted *Bear* sign.

Looking from Devizes Market Place into St. John's Street, late eighteenth century.
The New Hall is on the left with the Wool Hall to its right.

Old Park, Devizes

New Park House built in 1780 for James Sutton III by Wyatt and landscaped by Repton. The house was demolished in 1950.

of the two small sons. On the birth of the first potential heir the scene had been set for a prosperous line from James Sutton III at New Park and Sloper wrote in 1783, 'There was a large bonfire on the top of Roundway Hill .... and a feast in the booth for all his tennents', adding later 'but they paid for it very dear'. The two county Members of Parliament, Henry Penruddock and Ambrose Goddard, were god fathers, but the little boy died, as did his infant brother, and Sutton had no more sons.

Eleanor, one of the daughters of James Sutton III, called after her mother, married Thomas Grimston Estcourt, of Shipton Moyne and Ashley, near Tetbury, son of a member for Cricklade and High Sheriff of Wiltshire. Estcourt inherited New Park on his father-in-law's death in 1801, and continued the tradition of the family of providing a member for Devizes, being elected in 1805, and sitting until 1826, five years after Sloper's death. The latter would as a burgess be concerned as a voter (and participant in the borough members' hospitality) at all Addington's elections and five elections of T. G. Estcourt. James Sutton III, Addington and Estcourt were all Tories. William Willey, Sutton's uncle, member in 1747, is said to have been a Whig, and at some unrecorded time before that, in conversation with the great Whig Minister Robert Walpole, boasted that if he got into Parliament he would 'steer clear of all party and be an independent man'. To this the experienced Walpole allegedly retorted 'he must wear Will Pulteney's yoke or mine; and you will find mine the lighter'.[19] On the accession of George III in 1760 Willey is not recorded as being either Whig or Tory. Since 1698 Devizes burgesses had returned Whigs, as consistently as after 1760 they were to return Tories until the Reform Act of 1832.[20]

The influences of New Park's owners on the borough and late eighteenth century reformist thinking are illustrated in a History of English boroughs published in 1792:

> Devizes; Political character; the right of election .... is exercised by the Mayor, Aldermen and Common Council. The influence which prevails here is that of James Sutton of New Park .... brother-in-law of the Speaker. This town .... labours under the disadvantage .... of voting being limited to the body corporate and not extending to the people at large.[21]

Although in the 1760s the gentry were accustomed to having things their own way with no questions asked there must have been at least a degree of concern in the Sutton house (then in Long Street, Devizes) and at New Park, then the home of George Willey, the brother of M.P.

William, when, quoting the London newspapers *The Daily Gazette and The Public Ledger, The Gentleman's Magazine* for October 1760 published an unpleasant story under the heading 'Narrative of the facts relating to Ann Bell who died lately at Marylebone as is supposed by the shocking usage she met with some libertines in a bagnio'.[22] One of the alleged libertines was Willey Sutton, brother of James Sutton III and nephew of the two brothers George Willey of New Park, Mayor of Devizes a year earlier, and William Willey, rich East India Company Director and borough member. Sloper made no mention of this ugly rumour at the time, but in 1761 (probably in March) he wrote:

> Willy Sutton, eldest son of Prince Sutton Esq., was indicted and tryed ye Feb. 28 at Justice Hall, London, in ye Old Baily, for the willful murder of Ann Bell who dyed Saturday ye 30 Oct. 1760. N.b. he was acquitted – see *Universal Magazine* Vol. 28 – 143 page.[23]

Sloper made no judgement in his record on this event, and the respect of the burgesses of Devizes for the family at New Park appears to have been undiminished. They certainly re-elected William Willey to Parliament in the 1761 general election. Willey Sutton received New Park when his uncle William Willey died in 1765 and is shown as the owner on Dore's map of 1759. He died himself in 1775, apparently a bachelor, and New Park came to his younger brother, James Sutton III, elected to Parliament to follow his uncle William. The burgesses did not apparently invite Willey to represent them. (See Appendix D for the Willey/Sutton pedigree, and Appendix E for details relating to the trial of Willey Sutton.)

When Addington's short term as Prime Minister ended and Pitt took the reins of Government again, Sloper recorded, 'May 14 1804 the Right Honourable Henry Addington resigns his office of First Lord of the Treasurer and Chancelor of the Exchequer, and was succeeded in the said high office by the Right Honourable Wm. Pitt'. The Devizes burgesses were proud of their member Addington, and could find him useful:

> 1804 March 22. Mem. Wm. S. Hood was appointed to office in the Department of the Prohibited Bengal Warehouse .... I asked by letter by the favour of Mr. Addington which request he readily granted me.

Sloper and his fellow burgesses must have thought themselves close to the seats of power with Addington as Prime Minister, William Pitt a

The Univerſal Magazine
OF
Knowledge and Pleaſure:

CONTAINING

News,
Letters,
Debates,
Poetry,
Muſick,
Biography,
Hiſtory,

Geography,
Voyages
Criticiſm,
Tranſlations,
Philoſophy,
Mathematicks,
Huſbandry,

Gardening,
Cookery,
Chemiſtry,
Mechanicks,
Trade,
Navigation,
Architecture;

AND OTHER

Arts and Sciences;

Which may render it

Inſtructive and Entertaining

TO

GENTRY, MERCHANTS, FARMERS and TRADESMEN;

To which occaſionally will be added

An Impartial Account of *Books* in ſeveral Languages, and of the *State of Learning* in *Europe*:

Alſo

Of the STAGE New OPERAS PLAYS and ORATORIOS.

VOL. XXIII.

Publiſhed Monthly according to Act of Parliament
By *John Hinton* at the *King's Arms* in *Newgate Street London*.
Price Six Pence.
1752

George Sloper quotes extensively from *The Universal Magazine of Knowledge and Pleasure*.

1761 (39)

Fast Day Fryday
Febuary ye 13

Beau Richd Naish Esqr
Died at Bath Fryday
Feb: 13

Willy Sutton Eldest son
of Prince Sutton Esqr was
Indicted & Tryed
Saturday Feb: 28 - at Justice=Hall
London in ye old Baily
for the wilfull Murder
of Ann Bell who Dyed
Saturday August ye 30 last 1760
-113 — But he was Acquitted
See Universall Magazine
Voll. 28 - 143 Page
~~[illegible]~~

Generall Election Fryday
March ye 27

1761		
Febuary 9	M	2 - 14 - 0
10	Tuesday	2 - 0 - 0
11	Wend	2 - 4 - 0
12	Thursday	2 - 13 - 0
13	Fryday	2 - 3 - 0
14	Satt	4 - 0 - 0
		15 - 14 - 0
Feb. 16	Monday	4 - 12 - 0
17	Tuesday	2 - 0 - 0
18	Wend	2 - 8 - 0
19	Thursday	2 - 0 - 0
20	Fryday	2 - 6 - 0
21	Satt	4 - 2 - 0
		17 - 8 - 0
Feb. 23	Monday	4 - 3 - 0
24	Tuesday	2 - 4 - 0
25	Wend	2 - 2 - 0
26	Thursday	2 - 4 - 0
27	Fryday	2 - 8 - 0
28	Satt	4 - 0 - 0
		17 - 1 - 0
March 2	Monday	4 - 6 - 0
3	Tuesday	2 - 6 - 0
4	Wend	2 - 4 - 0
5	Thursday	2 - 3 - 0
6	Fryday	2 - 5 - 0
7	Satt	4 - 6 - 0
		17 - 10 - 0
March 9	Monday	2 - 8 - 0
10	Tuesday	2 - 8 - 0
11	Wend	2 - 4 - 0
12	Thursday	2 - 12 - 0
13	Fryday	2 - 5 - 0
14	Satt	5 - 0 - 0
		16 - 17 - 0
March 16	Monday	2 - 10 - 0
17	Tuesday	2 - 6 - 0
18	Wend	2 - 9 - 0
19	Thursday	3 - 0 - 0
20	Fryday	2 - 4 - 0
21	Satt	5 - 3 - 0
		18 - 2 - 0
March 23	Monday	4 - 13 - 0
24	Tuesday	2 - 0 - 0
25	Wend	2 - 0 - 0
26	Thursday	2 - 8 - 0
27	Fryday	2 - 4 - 0
28	Satt	2 - 15 - 0
		16 - 0 - 0
March 30	Monday	3 - 0 - 0

George Sloper notes the acquittal of Willey Sutton for the murder of Ann Bell.

visitor to New Park, and another Prime Minister, the Earl of Shelburne, at nearby Bowood. But there may be a hint of disapproval in 'the most noble John Henry Marquis of Lansdowne (eldest son of the late Marquis of Lansdowne who died Tuesday ye 6 of this instant May) was married ye 20 of this instant .... being 14 days after his father's death'.

In 1805 the Devizes burgesses decided to build a new Town Hall. It was opened on 2 November 1808 'with a ball and grand supper .... at the expense of the Mayor (Mr. Sm. Taylor) and corporation, who gave 5 guinies each'. Samuel Taylor, as Sloper wrote, was serving as Mayor for the fifth time. Samuel Adlam was another burgess with a long record of service to the borough, being Mayor in 1771, ten years before Sloper's first term, and holding the office on four subsequent occasions. He died in 1811 aged 78. Sloper wrote 'his property was supposed to be no less than £40,000'. In the early years of the nineteenth century several burgesses were mayors on more than one occasion – Stephen Hillman, a clothier, and James Gent, a brewer, four times, and Robert Bruges twice. The office must have been expensive to the holder, and prompted two lines of action by the borough council. In 1808 they elected six more burgesses to the Common Council. Sloper wrote:

> May 11 Friday Charter Day. Mr. Sml. Taylor chosen in Mayor .... 6 persons elected into the Corporation as Common Councilmen, viz.
>
> 1. Mr. Brabant, surgeon and man mid-wife and son-in-law to Wm. Hughes, attorney at law.
> 2. Mr. Everett, grocer.
> 3. Mr. Macfarley, Surgeon and Apothecary, and partner with Mr. Geo. Gibbs.
> 4. Mr. Clark, Druggist.
> 5. Mr. Geo. Heywood, Cheesemonger and son of Mr. Thos. Heywood.
> 6. Mr. Eldride at Old Park.

In 1814 the Council attempted to eject Stephen Powell, a former Mayor, as he had lived for four years in London and attended no Council meetings and by his 'absence the burden and duty of serving the office of Mayor has been rendered burdensome to other burgesses'.[24] Probably due to Salmon the Town Clerk's tact, Powell was not in fact ejected, though apparently he did not remain a Capital Burgess Councillor, taking the lesser role of Common Councilman. The burgesses must have been torn between appointing many more, which they certainly had power to do, thus diluting the quality of their membership and with the risk of placing a heavy burden on the few who had to serve as mayors repeatedly.

When Sloper's record ceases it is possible to determine at least some of his municipal activity during the 10 years to his death from Salmon's borough minutes. He continued to attend council meetings and to sit on committees, particularly those concerned with municipal property, but was not elected to the committee which arranged the building of the new Town Hall. He doubtless agreed with the rest of his colleagues to the election to Parliament of Joshua Smith and T. G. Estcourt in 1812, which was uncontested. He knew them well; he had been a recipient of game from the former and game and pineapples from the latter, and enjoyed the hospitality of both. However, the election of 1818 was different and produced a contest in which Sloper took an active part. Joshua Smith had died. The candidates were: T. G. Estcourt of New Park, whom the burgesses almost unanimously wanted to continue as member; John Pearse, who had no connection with Devizes, army clothing contractor from London and a Bank of England Director; William Salmon, Town Clerk and Deputy Recorder ('King Salmon'); and Wadham Locke, lawyer and banker, of Rowde Ford, whose election broadsheet described him thus;

> A native of your town of ancient and highly respectable families, connected with your town by a most respectable banking concern. He is an assiduous and just magistrate .... an excellent man in every situation of life .... his political sentiments are perfectly constitutional and he will be guided by conscientious principles.[25]

The election took place on 16 June 1818. Samuel Taylor, grocer and father of Admiral Joseph Needham Taylor, proposed 'King' Salmon, and this was seconded by Richardson, a Land Surveyor, who had counted James Sutton III amongst his clients. James Gent, the brewer who supplied Sloper with malt, proposed Pearse, which Stephen Neate, grocer in the High Street, seconded. William Hughes, a solicitor, struck an unusual note. He did not vote for Estcourt, the only burgess not to do so, and proposed his banking partner Wadham Locke. Sloper, perhaps for the first time in his life going against the majority of his burgess brethren, seconded Locke. When it came to the actual voting, each burgess having two votes, one for each seat, Estcourt recorded 25 (including Sloper's), Pearse 13, Salmon 10 and Wadham Locke 5. The Mayor, John Tylee, the Quaker banker of Broadleas Park, declared Estcourt and Pearse duly elected.[26] Salmon is thought only to have stood for election to split a possible vote in favour of Locke. Certainly if his 10 votes had been added to the latter's Locke would have been returned and Pearse defeated.

Sloper's departure from the strictly Tory line followed by his burgess colleagues ever since 1760, was probably due to the influence of his nephew, the capable and wealthy congregationalist minister, the Reverend Robert Sloper. However, three months after the election the latter died, though this did not mean that Sloper abandoned the somewhat anti-government position which he had taken at the 1818 election. The next year there was a by-election for one of the county seats, with nomination day at Devizes before the election day. Sir John Dugdale Astley opposed John Benett who had Wadham Locke as his party chairman. An unruly mob in support of Astley broke Sloper's windows, his support of Locke was not forgotten. Benett, like Locke a Parliamentary reformer, was elected.[27] The Government was becoming increasingly unpopular, and the arrest of 'Orator' Henry Hunt after the Peterloo Massacre, caused much resentment. Sloper knew his father well, and had recorded his death in August 1797, and would know of Hunt's friendship with his fellow-radical William Cobbett.[28] In January 1820 there was another general election and Sloper proposed Wadham Locke, though again he failed to win the seat.[29] Later when, in 1832 after the Reform Act, Locke was elected he was classed as a Whig. If Sloper in his old age never became a Whig, he was certainly sympathetic to their views, so had his windows brightly illuminated to celebrate the defeat of the Government over Queen Caroline's impeachment. This rejoicing the Tory Mayor and the rest of the corporation are said to have disapproved of and discouraged.[30] In his old age, therefore, Sloper was certainly capable of independent thought. Perhaps he was sad to see the former member Addington, now Viscount Sidmouth, and Home Secretary between 1812 and 1821, in the forefront of Governmental repressive measures.

References

1. W.R.O. 543/5, Churchwardens for St. Mary's Parish 1768–1806; 543/20, Poor Rate Book.
2. J. Waylen, *A History, Military and Municipal of the Ancient Borough of the Devizes* (1859), p.419. Thurman was a rich Bristol merchant.
3. W.R.O., G.20 1/37. Chamberlain's Accounts, 1778–1782.
4. *Ibid.*, G20/1/20, Borough Minute Book 1739–90.
5. S. and B. Webb, *English Local Government from the Revolution to the Municipal Corporations Act, Vol. 2,3. The Manor and the Borough, 2 pts* (London, 1908). Part 2, p.405.
6. *Encyclopaedia Britannica* (1953 edn.), Vol.III, p.290, article 'Borough'.
7. 21 Geo. III, C.36. The Commissioner's Minute Book 1781–8 is referenced under W.R.O. G.20/5/3.

8. *V.C.H.* Wiltshire, Vol.X, p.302.

9. *Ibid.*, p.313.

10. R. D. Gillman, *Annals of the Borough of Devizes* (Devizes, 1908), p.75. The Tylees, Quaker bankers and brewers, held the Devizes Mayoral chair five times between 1811 and 1825.

11. W.R.O. G.20/1/20.

12. *Ibid.*, G.20/1/37.

13. *Ibid.*, G.20/1/90, Oaths of Allegiance and Supremacy (1781–1830); B. H. Cunnington, *Some Annals of the Borough of Devizes: being a Series of Extracts from the Corporation Records 1535–1835* (2 vols. 1925–26) II, p.200.

14. W.R.O., G.20/1/20.

15. G. M. Trevelyan, *History of England* (1929), p.525, 526.

16. The Bridewell at Devizes was a county gaol and its iron-studded door can still be seen on a house in Bridewell Street.

17. W.R.O., G.20/5/3, Improvement Commission's Minute Book, 1781–8; B.H. Cunnington, op. cit., II, p.166.

18. W.R.O., G.20/1/21. Borough Minute Book F., 1790–1826.

19. J. Waylen, op. cit., p.405. Walpole was Prime Minister 1721–42. Though also a Whig, William Pulteney (1684–1764) subsequently created Earl of Bath, opposed him after 1728.

20. J. Waylen, op. cit., p.546–7.

21. T. H. B. Oldfield, *An entire and complete history, political and personal, of the boroughs of Great Britain* (London, 1792).

22. A bagnio can be a bath-house or a brothel: *Shorter Oxford English Dictionary* (3rd edition, 1956), p. 137.

23. For the trial of Willey Sutton see Appendix E. An account appeared in the February 1760 edition of *The Universal Magazine*.

24. W.R.O., G.20/1/21.

25. W.A.N.H.S. Library, Wiltshire Election Papers 1818–1868, Mr. Wadham Locke's address.

26. R. D. Gillman, op. cit., p. 25.

27. *Ibid.*

28. J. Waylen, op. cit., p.509.

29. R. D. Gillman, op. cit., p.26.

30. *Ibid.*

V End of a Long Life

George Sloper started his life with all the advantages of a good home, and due to diligence at his business and in the public affairs of his parish vestry and the borough of Devizes, he improved the status of his family in the town, dying a rich man, much respected not only by his colleagues on the Council but also by the major family in the district, that of the Suttons of New Park. Not many master bakers in a country town could claim to correspond with a Prime Minister as Sloper did with Addington. But despite what clearly was his close attention to business and public affairs, he never forgot his family, to which his record contains many references.

So we come to the last of Sloper's actions of significance in his long life, the making of his will, which William Salmon, the respected and long serving Town Clerk, known as 'King Salmon', and the most influential and experienced solicitor in Devizes, drafted for him. He signed it on 14 December 1819 before Salmon and his son William Wroughton, his successor as Town Clerk. There must have been a great deal of trust and respect between Sloper and Salmon; the latter had no doubt steered Sloper in his early days as councilman and Chamberlain, and in particular during his three years as Mayor of this ancient borough of which both were proud. Sloper was over ninety, highly respected and affluent, being worth about £10,000. A childless bachelor, he must have considered long whom to make his heir. As his main beneficiary he chose his great nephew, George Elgar Sloper, eldest son of the Reverend Robert Sloper, the wealthy founder of St. Mary's Congregational Church, who had attracted so many of the borough's leading citizens to the chapel in Northgate Street. This demonstrates the regard Sloper had for the family of his favourite brother, Benjamin, who had died in 1793.

George Elgar Sloper received under Sloper's Will the property on the north-east of the town known as Rotherstone, purchased at various times between 1775 and 1781, freehold land at Coate, tithes on both properties, land at Etchilhampton, and Sloper's own house, bought by his father over a hundred years previously, with the quondam bakehouse. George Elgar Sloper was also to receive 'all other copyholds and leaseholds', which would include a lease of Neck Mill and further land at Coate, copyhold of the manor of Bishops Cannings.

The major legacies were £3,000 to Nathaniel Elgar Sloper, second son of the Reverend Robert Sloper, £1,000 to his former apprentice Benjamin Noyes who was George Elgar Sloper's great-nephew, and £500 to the Revered Robert's married daughter, Ann Toomes. Minor legacies were £100 to the twelve-year-old Robert Leach 'son of my great-niece Mary, wife of Mr. Valentine Leach'. The Leaches, father and son, were the affluent re-builders of Devizes Castle. There were bequests to eight friends, remoter relations and a former servant, varying from 19 guineas to £10 and '£10 to each of my female servants, Martha Robbins and Jane Ellen', £50 to his miller at Neck Mill, £5 to 'my friend Mr. William Chandler for a ring', and £1 each to the 'two poor women in the old almshouses' of which Sloper was a trustee. Everything else, which would include money owed to him, and the furniture in the house in Sheep Street, was to go to George Elgar Sloper, who lived on, highly respected as both his father and his great-uncle had been, until 1865. It was his son, another George Elgar Sloper, who sold the old house in Sheep Street in 1883.

Sloper died on 21 November 1821, and was buried in St. John's Church, Devizes. Five days later the *Salisbury and Winchester Journal* reported; 'On Tuesday last died at the advanced age of 91. George Sloper Esq. of Devizes – he was almost the oldest member in the Corporation of that borough and had served the office of Mayor three times'. The will was proved on 9 January 1822. When Salmon drew up the wills of George Sloper's father and 'Bro. Ben' he recorded their occupation as bakers. But George Sloper had been Mayor, and the opening words of his Will read; 'this is the last Will and Testament of George Sloper of the Borough of Devizes in the County of Wiltshire – Gentleman'.

APPENDIX A

SLOPER'S PROPERTY ACQUISITIONS

Date	*Age*		*Capital Expenditure*
1770	40	'Bought late Cleave House of Hester Harris' for 'Began and entered on Neck Mill being out of it 19 years'.	£25
1771	41	Death of Samuel Sloper his father when he inherited the Sheep Street House, bakehouse and business, the latter probably including collectable debts to the business and ready cash. Thus he was in a position to buy the next year ...	
1772	42	'bought a leasehold estate at Coat att.'	£470
1773	43	'began building Painters house over the way'. (This was the junction of Bridewell Street and Morris Lane; later he was able to let it at 7 guineas p.a.)	
1775/81		Buys estate at Rotherstone between St. Mary's Church and Bath Road in three transactions; paid. ... (Later he could let part at £73 p.a. – see 1794.)	£1360 £200 £80
1775	45	(Opening of first Devizes Bank by James Sutton, Clothier, Wm. Leach, Snuff Maker, John Beavan a Quaker, and Richard Read Mayor of Devizes in 1777 and 1786.)	
1776	46	'Took Tinkfield bottom .... at £5.10s. p.a. for 12 years'. (This is adjacent to Neck Mill.) Renews Neck Mill waterwheel.	
1779	49	Lets land at Coate – land at £40 p.a. for 12 years, a barn at 17 guineas and house and garden at 6 guineas. Keeps nut trees, and wood for bakehouse faggots.	

Date	*Age*		*Capital Expenditure*
1780	50	Lets 'house over the way' at 7 gns. p.a. – see 1773. With 'bro Ben' takes Potterne Wood and Hare Mead for 10 years at £75 p.a. for bakehouse faggots. He kept the lease on until 1796 but stipulating that he could have 1 year's faggots and 2000 withies.	
1782	52	Lets '7 grounds barn and stables at Coat at ye yearly rent of 16 guineas' but keeps wood and fruit.	
1786	56	Buys copyhold estate at Nursteed from James Sutton at ...	£618
		Buys 2 tenements in Magpie Alley ...	£60
		Buys 'house and tenement' at ye corner going into ye Green' (at Junction of Hare and Hounds Street and Bridewell Street). In 1808 he builds a 'necessary house' there.	£60
		Buys 5¾ acres at Coate for ...	£225
1787	57	Gives £615 for copyhold of Manor of Bishops Cannings (James Sutton Lord of the Manor) – tenants in succession to be himself, nephew Rev. Robt. Sloper and great nephew Samuel, son of Rev. Robt.	£615
1789	59	Buys from Turnpike Trustees 'ye old road .... from Neck Mill and up Asheton Hill to corner of Broadway'.	£10 10s.
1790	60	Buys Shergold's estate at Coate, 109 acres (insures buildings for £300 with Royal Exchange Assurance Co. at 17/- premium p.a.).	£1320
		Builds 'kitchen and chamber over' at Rotherstone (see 1775/81).	
		Buys house from Thos. Adlam 'over way' – making four tenements – see 1773.	£85
1792	62	Buys another house in Magpie Alley – see 1786. (It lets at 3 guineas p.a.)	£45

Date	*Age*		*Capital Expenditure*
1793	63	Great nephew Samuel – see 1787 – having died pays for George Elgar Sloper, Samuel's brother, to be 'the third life' in the Bishops Cannings property	£90
1794	64	Lets Rotherstone and house as nursery gardens at £72 p.a. (Attends Bishops Cannings manorial court as a copy-holder.)	
1795	65	Buys 50 acres at Tinkfield – see 1776. Pays	£2000
1796	66	Lets $4^1/_2$ acres at Coate, house and garden at 12 guineas p.a. and a load of barley; gives up Potterne Wood.	
1808	78	Lets 2 grass fields at Rotherstone for 40 guineas for 5 years. Buys further land at Coate.	£1100
1809	79	Buys leasehold at Nursteed, which with repairs cost	£180

APPENDIX B

SLOPER'S PUBLIC AND MUNICIPAL PROGRESS

Date	*Age*	
1730	–	(Born, youngest son of Samuel Sloper, burgess and baker, Devizes.)
1754	24	Joins Gardeners Club.
1755	25	Joins Bear Club.
1762	32	Elected Overseer of the Poor, St. Mary's Parish.
1768	38	Chosen Mayor's Constable.
1770	40	Elected by St. Mary's Parish Surveyor of Highways.
1772	42	Chosen a feofee of lands of St. Mary's Church.
1775	45	Elected Churchwarden for St. Mary's (which post he held until he became Mayor).
1777	47	Elected Chamberlain (i.e. Treasurer) of the Borough (held post until Mayor).
1779	49	'Chosen Warden of ye old Almshouse'.
1780	50	Served on borough's Grand Jury at its Quarter Sessions and elected Foreman; nominated by Act of Parliament an Improvement Commissioner (21 Geo III).
1781	51	Elected Mayor of Devizes. Chairman of Improvement Commissioners.
1784	54	Becomes a trustee of the Green, Nursteed, and Rowde Turnpike Road.
1791	61	Elected Mayor for a second time.
1792	62	Again elected Chamberlain (holds post for 4 years).
1800	70	Elected Mayor for the third time.
1809	79	Elected Mayor, declined, fined £5 (usually the fine was £30).
1813	83	Ditto – fined £10.
1814	84	Ditto – fined £15.

Date	*Age*	
1818	88	At a General Election, active politically on behalf of reformer Wadham Locke, whom he proposes as borough member.
		Voting – T. G. Estcourt 25; W. Salmon 10; John Pearse 18; W. Locke 5
1819	89	At a County election, Locke Chairman for John Benett, reformer, who defeats Sir J. D. Astley. The latter's supporters smash Sloper's windows.
1820	90	A borough election. Sloper again proposing Locke.
		Voting – Estcourt 21; Pearse 16; Locke 7
1820	90	Shows Whig sympathies on the Government's failure over Queen Caroline's impeachment, and illuminates his house in triumph despite the disapproval of the Mayor (Wm. Hughes) and Corporation. His windows are again broken.
1821 Nov.	91	Death.

APPENDIX C

THE TRIAL OF WILLEY SUTTON

Willey Sutton was the elder son of Prince Sutton, well-to-do clothier living in Long Street, Devizes. The Suttons were a well established clothier family, James Sutton I, 'of Devizes, Clothier', being Mayor five times between 1697 and 1712. His son James Sutton II, born 1678, also a clothier, was Mayor in 1715, 1718 and 1730, and married Anne Prince, their offspring including the eldest son, Prince Sutton, born 1701, Mayor in 1744, and – a definite advance in County status – High Sheriff of the county in 1762. He married Mary Willey, whose bachelor brothers were George Willey of New Park, Mayor in 1749, and William, well-to-do London merchant (probably in the cloth trade), an East India Company Director and Member for Devizes between 1754 and 1756.

The offspring of the marriage of Prince Sutton, Mayor and High Sheriff, and Mary Willey, were the elder son Willey Sutton, called after his mother's family, James Sutton III, and three daughters.

In 1760 the death of a girl in London, allegedly at the hands of Willey Sutton, meant an inquest and, depending on the inquest jury's verdict or an 'information' laid before a magistrate, his trial on a charge of murder or manslaughter would be likely to follow. The girl died, for whatever reasons, in October of that year, as Sloper noted in his record.

The facts, undisputed at the inquest held before the Marylebone Coroner and a jury of 23 and at Willey's subsequent trial, were that he and one Sir William Fowler took two girls, described as Ladies of the Night, to Haddock's Bagnio near Covent Garden. Sutton stayed two nights there with Ann Bell, and Sir William with Mary Young. Ann Bell, who came of a good family from Norwich, used several names. Captain Holland of the Norfolk Militia interested himself in her case and probably knew her father; he was certainly in correspondence with him after her death. Some weeks elapsed between the time that Sutton and Sir William spent the two nights with the girls at the bagnio, and during that time Ann Bell became very ill, alleging to various friends and servants that Sutton had stabbed her between the buttocks with a penknife, thus causing her illness. A lot of people believed this story and according to the *London Gazette* there was much public unease about the affair. However, the inquest jury acting, it seems on medical evidence that Ann's death was due to a fever and not to her injuries, brought in a verdict of 'natural causes'. This did not end the matter nor in particular did it satisfy Captain Holland, who went to see Sir John Fielding, the famous London Magistrate and founder of the Bow Street Runners, who, as Sloper would remember, had been in Devizes in 1768. Holland did not initially ask for action against Sutton, and as the law then stood it was necessary for one who complained of a crime to 'lay an information'. This Holland did not do, so Fielding did nothing. The public disquiet continued, and after correspondence with Ann's father, Holland did lay an information, though before having served it on Sutton he took it to Sutton's uncle, almost certainly William Willey, the Devizes M.P. His purpose in doing this is obscure – perhaps he was hoping to find a way of avoiding further scandal. This came to nothing. He then published the facts as he saw them, and Sutton attempted to silence him by unsuccessfully suing for libel in the King's Bench Division. Eventually the information was served and Sutton was arrested. At the trial Mary Young said she knew of no injury. Sir William Fowler could not give evidence as he had died in Germany. The doctors restated their view that the injury was not the cause of death. There was an acquittal accordingly.

The scandal did not, however, inhibit the public lives of Sutton's father Prince, or his uncle William. In the year of the trial William Willey was returned Borough Member by unanimous vote. The year after it Prince Sutton became High Sheriff. Willey Sutton never married, so far as is known. His family did not disown him, the eldest son, and he was living at New Park in 1775 when Sloper noted his death.

APPENDIX D

PROSOPOGRAPHY

Note: The persons mentioned in this Appendix are all referred to in the text.

ADLAM	Samuel (1733 – 1811). A clothier in 1783, a maltster in 1797. Family prominent in Devizes since early 18th century. Close contemporary of Sloper's but senior to him on the Council. Four times Mayor. Property owner. Wealthy. Sloper estimated Adlam worth £40,000 on his death aged 78 in 1811.
ANSTIE	Two branches of this family. One made snuff, grinding it in two windmills on the castle mound in partnership with William Leach (q.v.). John Anstie a clothier at the more sophisticated end of the trade – Sloper: 'May 12 1788 Mr. John Anstie the Great clothier keeps 300 looms at work. But the French War bankrupted him in 1792.' Not a burgess.
BAYLY	Francis (1736 – 96). An Attorney. Mayor 1788 when signs an address of congratulations to William Pitt.
BRABANT	Dr. R. H., of Sandcliffe House. Surgeon/Midwife. Elected a burgess in 1808, never Mayor. Said to be the origin of Casaubon in George Eliot's *Middlemarch.*
BRUGES	Robert. A draper (1783). Twice Mayor, died 1815 – M. I. in St. John's.
CLARK	John Singleton. A druggist. Elected a burgess 1808 (Sloper notes all appointments to the Council that year when the Senior Burgesses were complaining that the Mayoralty should be more widely shared). Mayor four times, the last at the time of the Reform Acts 1832 – 35 when he took the lead to retain two M.P.s for Devizes with success.
ELDRIDGE	William, of Old Park, Devizes. Elected burgess 1808 (Sloper spells his name Eldride, but gives no occupation).

ESTCOURT	Thomas Grimston, of New Park. M.P. Devizes. Married Eleanor daughter of James Sutton III (q.v.). Addington's brother-in-law. Received acclaim for his investigation into the prison conditions of 'Orator' Hunt. Sold New Park 1836. Later M.P. for Oxford University. Died 1853.
EVERETT	William. A grocer in 1809. Twice Mayor.
FIGGINS	Matthew. Maltster and brewer. Partnership 'Figgins and Gent'. Family in Devizes since 17th century. Twice Mayor. Supplied Sloper with malt for home brewing.
FLOWER	John (1713 – 1787). Five times Mayor.
GARTH	Charles. M.P. and Recorder, of Brownston House. Son of John Garth who had held these offices (M. I. in St. Mary's). Took 'Chiltern Hundreds' on receiving a Government appointment.
GENT	James. Brewer in partnership with Matthew Figgins (q.v.). Four times Mayor. In 1797 'his income might be deemed to be a large one'. Sold Sloper malt. Died 1829.
GENT	Matthew. A clothier. Never Mayor. Married a sister of William Salmon (q.v.). Chamberlain with Sloper.
GENT	Harry. Chamberlain 1792 – 1806 but not Mayor. Still a burgess in 1821.
GIBBS	George. 'The Inoculator'. Born 1813. Three times Mayor. Made 'Justice' (permanent Magistrate) for Devizes. Practised with Dr. Macfarlane (q.v.) in the Market Place, with the statue of Aesculapius on the facade of his house.
HALCOMB	William. Landlord at *The Bear*, where bankrupt; previously at *King's Arms*.
HEYWOOD	George. A cheesemonger. Elected burgess in 1808.
HILLMAN	Stephen. A clothier (1783). Elected burgess in same year (1777) as Sloper. Four times Mayor. Of Greystone House (as tenant of James Sutton III).

HUGHES	William. Solicitor and later banking partner with Wadham Locke (q.v.) in 1829. Three times Mayor. A reformer.
INNES	The Rev. Edward (1712 – 1778). Curate at Devizes when stirs the mob against the Wesleys (1747). Inducted as Rector 1774.
LEACH	William. Snuff maker. Partner with Anstie (q.v.). Elected a burgess 1771 with Sloper. Never Mayor.
LOCKE	Wadham III (1780 – 1835). Solicitor and Banker (Locke Hughes & Co.) of Brownston House after Mr. Garth (q.v.). His father a solicitor and his mother a daughter of James Sutton, the banker clothier of Town End. At 19 ensign in Loyal Devizes Volunteers. A reformer; after two failures to get the burgesses to elect him M.P. eventually succeeded in 1832 under the new franchise.
LONG	Sir James Tilney, baronet, of Draycott. M.P. Devizes 1780 – 88 when stood for the county and succeeded by Joshua Smith (q.v.).
LUDLOW	William. A snuff maker, of Hillworth House (the Folly) which he built. Bankrupt by 1814.
MACFARLANE	Dr. Charles. Partner with Dr. Gibbs (q.v.). Elected burgess 1808. Never Mayor (Sloper – 'Macfarley').
POWELL	Stephen. Maltster. Lived, Sloper says, 'over the way'. Twice Mayor. Was criticised for living outside Devizes and not taking his full share of Council Activity.
READ	Richard. Elected burgess 1777, with Sloper. Mayor 1785.
READ	William. Mayor 1776. Died 1779.
RICHARDSON	Richard. A surveyor. Elected burgess 1780; active politically 1818.

SALMON	William II. Son of William Salmon I and father of William Wroughton Salmon, all three attorneys and Town Clerks of Devizes. Very influential and popular, holding office (inter alia) as Clerk of the Peace at Borough Quarter Sessions, Deputy Recorder, Clerk to the Court of Record; in 1780 Secretary to the County Reform Committee; in 1785 Under-Sheriff to James Sutton III (q.v.), Clerk to the Improvement Commissioners; Secretary to the Wiltshire Fire Insurance Society; Captain-Commandant of the Devizes Loyal Volunteers 1799. Elected a burgess in 1770 and Chamberlain 1803 – 15. Known as King Salmon. Died 1826, when the Council voted an address of appreciation. M. I. in St. John's.
SMITH	Joshua, of Erlestoke. M.P. Devizes 1788 to 1818, when died. A liberal contributor to borough funds.
SUTTON	James III, of New Park. Addington's brother-in-law. M.P. Devizes 1765 – 80. High Sheriff (as his father had been) 1785. His daughter married T. G. Estcourt (q.v.). Died 1801.
SUTTON	James, of Town End. Banker and clothier.
TAYLOR	Samuel. 1736 – 1818. Fives times Mayor. Known as Captain Taylor and active on the Council to the year of his death, when 'the father of the Corporation'.
TYLEE	John. A Quaker and brewer. Mayor three times after 1811.
TYLEE	Thomas. Mayor 1815 and 1824.
WHATLEY	George. Landlord at *The Bear*. Bankrupt 1754. Died 1769 still 'of the *Bear*'.
WHITFIELD	Thomas. (1732 – 1810). A draper. Sloper a customer. Twice Mayor.
WILLIAMS	Henry. Sloper says '1766 Mr. Henry Williams Mayor' – his only mayoralty.

INDEX